RUTH LEE

PATTERN ON
THE KNITTING MACHINE

B.T. Batsford Ltd, London

Acknowledgement

My thanks are due to all those who helped me slave over knocking the book into shape, especially my long-suffering partner, Michael Pearce, who typed all my handwritten script on to the word processor.

ISBN 0 7134 5914 X

Typeset by Servis Filmsetting Ltd
and printed in Great Britain
by The Bath Press, Bath
for the publishers
B.T. Batsford Ltd
4 Fitzhardinge Street
London W1H 0AH

Illustrations by Ruth Lee
Photographs by Steve Thomas, Andrew Morris,
Martin Hewer and Howard Guest.

CONTENTS

Introduction

This is intended to be a working manual on techniques in patterned and decorative machine knitting, which adopts a creative approach backed by a thorough exposition of method, including detailed examples. The book assumes that the reader has some experience with the machine. It is not a text for the complete beginner, although elementary principles are outlined where this assists in explaining more elaborate methods. Many illustrative examples are provided.

It is hoped that the reader will participate and be encouraged to develop and build on these examples, and will be sufficiently inspired by them to work out new ideas of her or his own.

As for myself – I started out as a would-be fabric-print designer, but found that I was unhappy simply working with flat pattern. I wanted to be able to change the surface itself, to design with the texture and feel of the material, to raise the surface in places. Knitting seemed a natural progression, given my love for pattern and colour.

I hope I succeed in transmitting some of my enthusiasm for my work, and that the book will help you to create all the things you have perhaps considered making but lacked the confidence or the know-how to try. Have a go – you could easily become a lifelong addict.

Creative machine knitting! The very phrase conjures up experimental surfaces of knit which combine unusual applications of colour, pattern and texture using one or more techniques. Functional considerations work alongside aesthetics in designs for clothing, accessories and furnishings, or simply decorative pieces (see fig 1).

Each project will throw up problems (which hopefully you will view as challenges). Many of these you will have met and overcome before, if you are an experienced machine-knitter, but new designs naturally mean new challenges requiring that you find new solutions. The process of discovery is one of the great pleasures to be had from any creative work, and this applies as much with machine-knitting as any other field of endeavour.

Fig 1. *Strip coat. Plain knit wool base with knitted-in patterned strips, using a mixture of wools, cottons, chenilles, slub and bouclé yarn.*

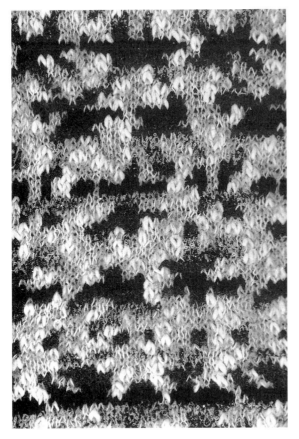

Fig 2. *Double-bed Jacquard knitted over a 24-stitch repeat in a range of small scale patterns using wool, slub cotton, fine mohair mixes and industrial weight lurex.*

Since the book is intended to be inspirational rather than prescriptive, it will, I hope, encourage the same pioneering approach that has sustained my enthusiasm for many years and which continues to keep the subject an exciting one for me. It should give you the confidence to try out and develop your own design ideas, and to take the problems in your stride.

This book is limited to variations on a simple knit structure consisting of one row Purl, one row Plain, and excludes experiments with more complex stitch structures (with the exception of double-bed Jacquard). Thus I have concentrated mainly on varieties of stocking-stitch, for example Intarsia and 2-colour stranded knitting, alongside Partial-knit methods (see figs 2, 3, 4, 5, 6 and 7).

The types of images and designs included in this book tend to read more clearly on knits with a simple structure, where texture is achieved by way of contrasting yarns, such as rayon, mohair, cotton and silk, rather than elaborate stitch technique. You should be aware, though, that the use of various stitch-effects generates many more possibilities.

Such methods as Multi-colour Tuck stitch, or Knitweave in combination with patterned knit, open up many more possibilities, but are outside the scope of this book.

Some of the techniques included show ways of manipulating the surface of the knitting to produce decorative effects, such as Pleating, Appliqué, and slitted surfaces, but again the emphasis is on simple structure and surface pattern.

Throughout the book I will try to encourage the concept of the knitting-machine as being the means to an end – the tool whereby your ideas become finished pieces. Learn to control the machine and

Right **Fig 3.** *Co-ordinating double-bed Jacquard patterns with a wide striped rib. Cotton, wool, 'Geneve' (80% acrylic 20% nylon) from Atkinson.*

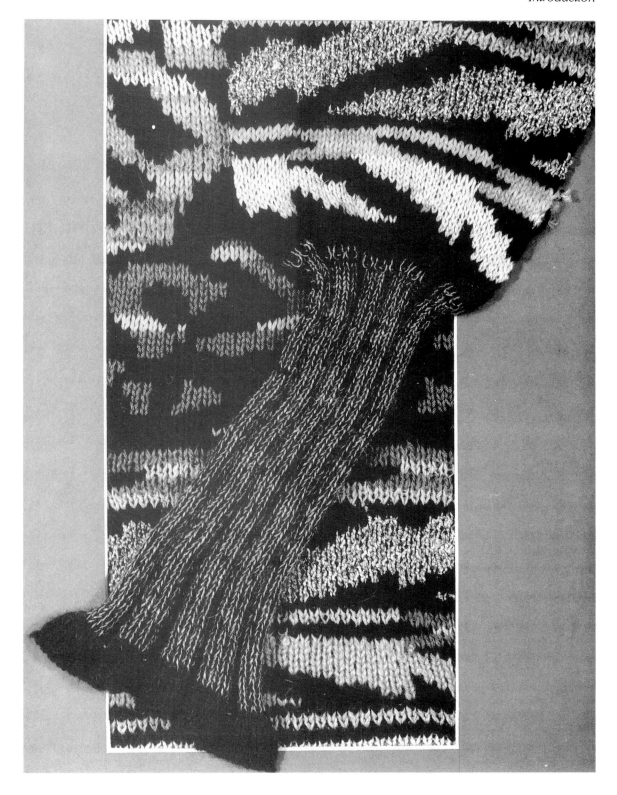

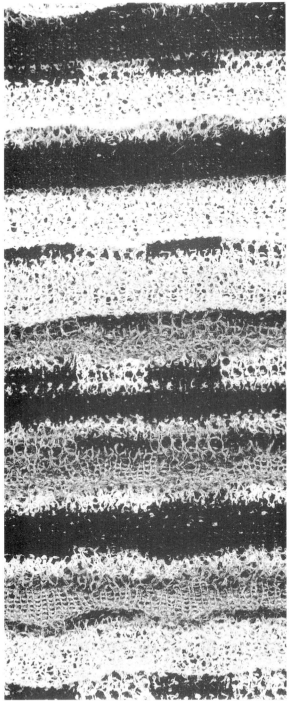

Fig 4. *Ripple technique Jacquard in fine synthetic yarns.*

Fig 5. *Patterned (single-bed) and slitted surface with knitted-in bobbles and a plain-knit underlay (purl side facing). Chenilles, rayons, lurex, cotton mixes and wool.*

have confidence in it and you will have overcome the first obstacle to designing and producing your own, original, work.

The more you understand the workings of your machine the easier it is to correct errors, or at least to know why a particular sample went wrong. If you feel confident that you can cope with all eventualities (and we all of us, however experienced, make mistakes) you will be much happier about trying out new ideas.

If something doesn't work out too well the first time, you will feel far less despondent if you have an idea of why the problem cropped up, and how to fix it. It may be a simple matter such as broken stitches caused by the wrong tension for a particular yarn, but if you aren't familiar with your equipment, this sort of thing can be very frustrating.

It is most important to be able to assess what to do when a piece has gone wrong. Often, time can be saved (in the long run) by scrapping the piece and starting again rather than spending fruitless hours trying to salvage a sample that has gone too far wrong for redemption.

This last point applies perhaps more with bad creative decisions than technical hitches. Even so, spending ten minutes unpicking faulty rows when you are only five minutes into the work is clearly bad practice (unless by doing so you learn something). This may be an obvious point to make, but it does happen, and experience and familiarity will stop you from falling into that particular trap.

Remember that patience, practice, confidence (and a sense of humour) are of paramount importance on the road to becoming a successful creative machine-knitter. Don't be frightened to take chances, since the worst thing that can happen is that you fail. You will at least learn from this and be more likely to succeed the next time. Let your imagination loose and you will begin to see results.

Don't let your knitting machine inhibit or intimidate you (perhaps easier said than done). There will come a time when *you* will be in control of *it* rather than vice-versa. While you should have respect for the equipment, don't have too timid an approach to using it. These machines are very robust and unless you are really heavy-handed or extremely careless the worst you will do is break or bend a few needles.

However, here is a cautionary tale. Some years ago during a very busy period producing rushed orders, I failed to check that the needle-bed extension-rail was fitted on my machine (I was using a Brother KH830 at the time). A hasty and ill-considered attempt to park the carriage on the non-existent rail resulted in its

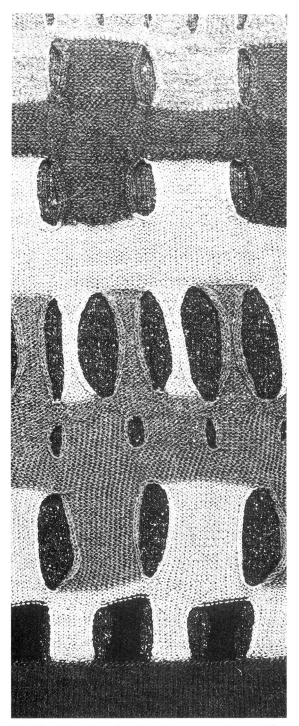

Fig 6. *Plain-knit slitted surface using the purl face of the knitting, in cotton and wool.*

Fig 7. *Knitweave slits, using wools, boucles and mohair.*

avoid leaving claw-weights and tools behind the machine close to the yarn cones – they will tangle with the yarn, which will then pull tight and break.

Try to anticipate in your mind how calamities such as the one described above may come about, and take avoiding action. Don't leave odd needles in the forward position where they can tear clothes or cause personal injury to yourself or others.

Generally the more experienced and practical you are the less likely you are to be inhibited by your machine. You soon realise if you are trying to do things that the machine cannot safely cope with.

This has always been my philosophy toward machine knitting. Disaster is occasionally snatched from the jaws of success, as it were, but this can be regarded as part of the adventure, and a provider of valuable experience. Taking chances, and practice, will help you to evaluate why one sample has worked while another hasn't.

Experience will also tell you whether a failed idea can be improved, or if you should discard it and move on to something else, or if a design idea has been developed as far as it can be – a conclusion which is often far from obvious. Perhaps the sample in question is unsuitable for the present purpose from a design point of view, but could work in a different context, or be a starting point for another project. To deal competently with decisions of this nature, you must develop the artist in yourself.

You may find it worthwhile, as I do, to keep the majority of your samples for future reference. Note down details such as tension, method used, number of stitches, type of yarn and its supplier, and any other unusual details you think might be useful.

Write the details in a notebook together with a reference number, then write the number on a cardboard tie-on label and attach this to the sample. Then you can put the samples all together in a box or bag and keep the notes themselves somewhere safe. It can be infuriating to be inspired by an old sample and to have no idea how to go about reproducing it.

It is also worth building up reference material from which you can obtain inspiration either for producing your own ideas, or adapting existing patterns.

Collect magazine cut-outs, colour charts (from paint shops or artists' suppliers), postcards, and snips of fabric, yarn or paper.

Colour is one of the most important ingredients of a successful design. The same pattern can take on quite different characteristics, depending upon the combination of colours being used – for example

describing a trajectory through the air (which rapidly turned blue) and meeting a stone flagged floor.

The expensive consequence of this incident was a panic visit to a repair-shop and a missed deadline. Carpetting was purchased soon afterwards.

Such happenings generally occur as a result of carelessness, forgetfulness and/or trying to do too many things at once. Make a check on all the important aspects of your equipment and workbench on a daily basis, and keep things tidy. For example

Fig 8. *Lace and plain-knit slitted surfaces using fine crochet cotton, rayons, and a Botany wool.*

Fig 9. *Pattern graph for an electronic machine.*

subtle blends of quiet shades or strong contrasting hues.

In order to achieve a greater fluency in the use of colour, and subsequently in your knit design, there is no real substitute for practical application and handling of colour through the use of paints, inks, and pastels for example, or directly, with the blending and knitting of yarns.

Observing and analysing how other artists and designers have used colour will complement your own 'hands-on' experience. Your awareness of new possibilities will be sharpened and the ideas can then be directly applied to your knit designs. Another source of information comes in the form of the trade magazines used in the fashion and textiles industry, such as *International Textiles*. In them colour combinations and styles are forecast for coming seasons.

Where to begin? You may find the task all too daunting, feeling that your colour sense is not particularly well developed, and you may be unsure how to make headway. In order of priority, you will need a source of information for colour ideas, a method of recording this information, and an understanding of how to use the information to enable you to design and produce actual knitted pieces.

A quick way of beginning to understand colour is to use a colour notebook and a set of reference files. Start and maintain a collection of postcards, photographs, magazine cuttings, fabric and yarn ends whose colour especially appeals to you. Colour charts from paint shops and artists' suppliers can also be useful in this context.

Keep adding to your collection. I find that the most convenient way of storing these items is to use the box-files sold by office stationers, but you may have your own ideas. What you use doesn't matter as long

Fig 10. *Two-colour single-bed patterned knit. Leaf design knitted in a variety of solid and mixed colours (dark blues and white) including cottons, slub mixes, fancies and bouclé yarns.*

Fig 11. *Two-colour, single-bed patterned knit.*
Leaf design knitted in cottons, wools and chenilles.

as it allows for easy removal and replacement of items for comparing colours.

It is also good practice to sort out some sort of filing system for the various main colours – all reds, yellows, or all dark (or light) colours, all soft muted colours, and so on. Again it is important to be able to isolate individual colours for comparison, so it is not

16

Fig 12. *Two-colour, single-bed patterned knit. Leaf design in smooth, fine wools (creamy white and dark blue).*

Fig 13. *Graph for leaf design.*

advisable to fix things permanently to paper sheets, for instance.

Information for imagery, pattern and texture can be stored in much the same way. Chapter 3 suggests ways in which you can utilise this for 2-colour knitting, while the chapter on Intarsia (Chapter 4) shows methods of working with more pictorial images alongside geometric patterns.

Record patterns and shapes, along with colour, in sketchbooks or with a camera, together with anything

else that could be used for information and cross-referencing at the start of each new project.

Themes for pattern and texture depend very much on individual tastes and requirements. Many diverse examples are suggested in Chapters 3 and 4.

It is well worth collecting as many current shade cards as possible. Addresses can usually be found in any of the many knitting periodicals. Also visit knitting fairs and trade shows when they occur in your area. This will give you a good chance to see new yarns at first hand, as well as other new developments.

If you buy odd balls of yarn, keep the label and a snippet of the yarn for future reference. It also helps to make small knitted samples, making notes of suitable tensions and any potential problems for both single and double-bed techniques – not all yarns will work for both.

Fig 14. *Examples of various yarns currently available to the machine knitter.*

A selection of currently available yarns is catalogued in photographic form alongside a series of examples knitted in various combinations to the same pattern (figs 14 and 38). A list of suppliers is given at the end of the book.

Chapter 9 looks in greater depth at the main qualities of some of the most popular yarns, and suggests suitable uses and applications for garments and apparel generally.

Throughout the book I have included samples and graphs together with instructions demonstrating the main methods. Each chapter builds from the most simple interpretation of a technique through to more complex variations. Much of the sampling makes reference to specific brand-names of yarn. This is meant as a guide. Try out combinations that seem suitable, comparing weights and qualities with the given examples if problems arise.

I hope you will use each example as a guide and they will offer encouragement to the point where you can apply your own ideas and adaptations. I suggest that you work systematically through the samples given in each chapter. But it is worth referring to methods in other sections, if you feel they are appropriate, until you gain enough confidence to manipulate the techniques to your own ends. At this point you will no doubt be itching to make your own original pieces and disregard my ideas in favour of your own.

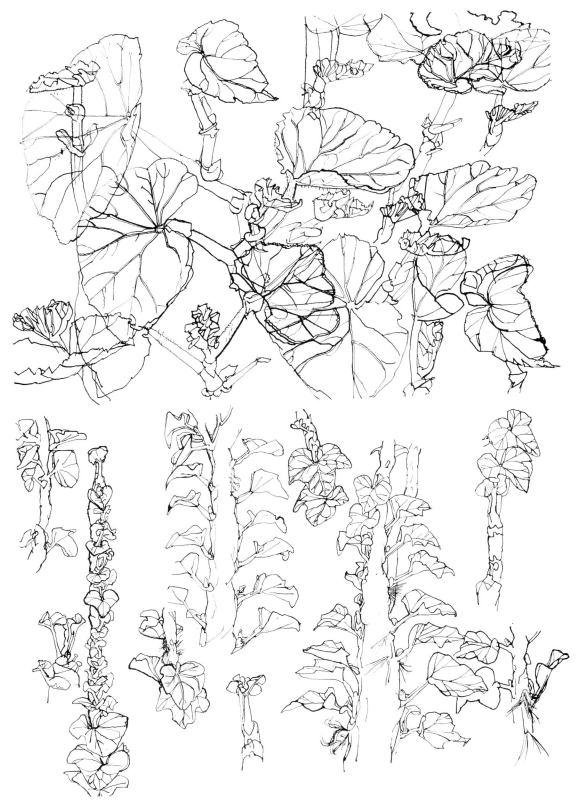

Fig 15. *Example of a page from a sketch-book showing ideas which can be the basis for new designs.*

19

CHAPTER 1
Single-bed patterned knitting

Single-bed patterned knitting is a popular method of working because of its underlying simplicity of technique and structure. It invites experimentation and can have many applications for both wearables and furnishing pieces. Also it is a quick and efficient method of producing colourful areas of all-over flat pattern in various repetitive sequences. These can either be developed in their own right or in combination with other techniques such as slitted surfaces, ribbing, and partial knitting, producing many new designs (see fig 16).

It is important to understand the inherent limitations and possibilities of each successive technique, and then to consider the implications for practical design work, whether the technique is being used alone or in association with another method.

The main feature of this method is the production of two (or sometimes three) colour-in-a-row patterns where the colours not in use are stranded across the back of the knitting. These strands are known as 'floats', and they result in the knitting having only a limited amount of elasticity – an important aspect which must be taken into account at the design stage.

Experimenting with the pattern card

Throughout the sampling in this section, I have treated colour as a matter of strong tonal contrast – limiting the colour content and exploring the relationship between light, dark, and mid-tones in the patterns. These mid-tones are often just neutral in colour, for example browns, greys and creams, in conjunction with dark grey and white.

Single light and/or dark hues have also been used, with the emphasis placed on variation within the

Fig 16. *Section of machine-knitted jacket, combining single bed 2-colour patterned knit with a 5 plain-5 purl 2-colour rib, and plain knitting over a patterned underlay. Wools, cottons, cotton slub with a cotton/linen mix.*

pattern to produce solid shape, linear outlines, or the appearance of tonal variation (chequerboard, close stripe, etc). Sources of inspiration for tonal and monochrome work include the following:

- Resist-dyed fabrics from India, Pakistan and Nigeria, characterized by single-colour designs.
- Javanese batik from the nineteenth century, which show dark browns, sepias, or shades of blue.
- Bakuba raffia cloth from Zaire, in black and ochres.
- English resist-printing of the late eighteenth century, using shades of indigo.
- English copper-plate printed textiles (late eighteenth century) using single colours, executed in fine line and subtly produced effects of light and shade in red, blue, black and sepia.

These copper-plate printed fabrics are most interesting to look at, and could be a useful source of design ideas generally, apart from the monochromatic theme that I am dealing with in this section. The images include floral patterns featuring blooms and grasses both common and exotic, peacocks, classical ornaments, and so on.

Inspiration can also be gleaned from:

- Ceramic patterns such as Willow pattern, Wedgwood's Jasperware or Ancient Greek vases featuring classical imagery in black and white or green and white.
- Patterns from nature; marble, animal and plant markings, tree-bark, wood-grain, ripples and swirls in water, cloud formations.
- Old, faded sepia-tinted photos, or indeed black-and-white photos generally.

It is always worth looking at traditional knitwear from various parts of the world (try your library for pictures). Much of this work employs few colours, since only a very limited range of dyes were available in the past when the traditional themes first appeared, so most of the creative effort went into producing an elaborate pattern.

To mention a few examples, there is Sanquhar – featuring fine checked patterns using blocks, diamond shapes and smaller patterns echoing woven tweed in two contrasting colours. A fine yarn is used to show the patterns off to great advantage. Sanquhar knitting comes from the Scottish Borders, around Dumfries.

Icelandic Lopi yoked sweaters use several shades of natural yarn on the pattern yoke, but feature only two colours per row. Alternatively, traditional ski jackets from Norway in black and white use contrast-

Fig 17. *Collage of images taken from half-timbered buildings as source material.*

ing small, all-over patterns, and bands of bolder pattern, such as the traditional star motif. Norwegian designs were generally worked in two colours, with the pattern silhouetted against a light background. Swedish traditional caps and stockings are also worked in contrasting shades of red, blue and white.

Natural colours are not necessarily obtained by dying. For example, the colours obtained from Shetland sheep-fleece vary from a very dark brown through russets and greys to off-white. These yarns are still very popular with knitters, as are yarns spun from the fleece of Jacobs sheep.

I have included a collection of patterns derived from photos of half-timbered buildings (see fig 17). These work into a 24-stitch repeat system, but in fact the individual limit of repeat of some of the patterns could be suited to machines with a smaller or wider repeat size.

It is perhaps beneficial to start by working with a ready-made collection of patterns, each of which has a distinct characteristic. The advantage of this is that each will stand by itself as a design, but would also work with other patterns from the group, so allowing the for development of many different images.

Further on in the book I will suggest ways in which you can develop your own personal collection of images suited to this type of knitting. The designs in Fig 49 are all capable of being knitted in a variety of pattern-repeat sizes on many different machines, from the electronic type to the push-button pattern devices, as well as the standard 24-stitch repeat machines.

Single-bed samples

First punch out or draw on to electronic machine paper the graphs illustrated in figs 18–27.

Knit through each pattern in dark grey and white only (or any other light/dark combination). Then try out a series of simple variations, such as exchanging foreground for background colour for either the complete pattern repeat, or specific sections of the design.

Practice elongating the pattern, again for part or whole of the pattern, swapping background for foreground colour at intervals. Lock the card and knit several repeats of the same row. Alternatively rewind the card to a new starting point, knit a few rows, then rewind the card again. Intersperse a few rows of plain knitting in the main colour only, or as stripes to divide the pattern into bands.

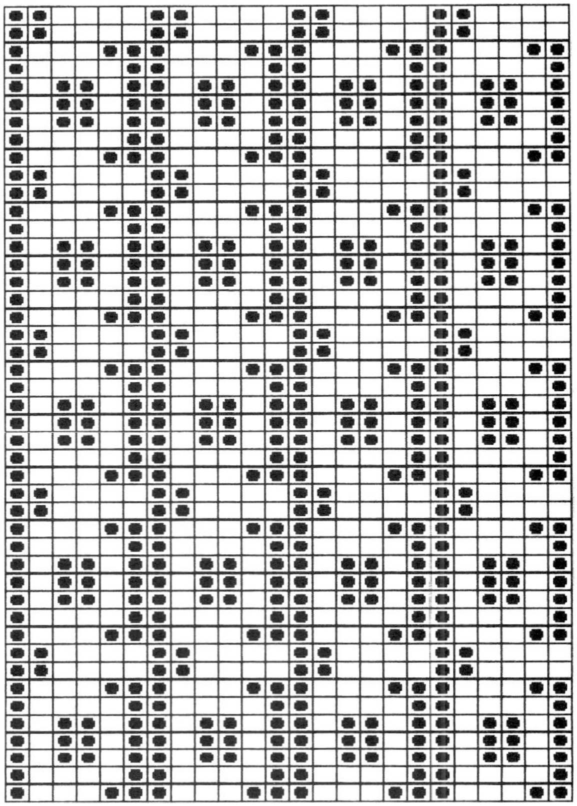

Fig 18. *Pattern graph A.*

The following samples show you exactly how to do all these things. Work through as many different ideas as possible, making a note of the variations against a numbered sample. I use blank tie-on price tags to record this information, together with the tension setting and number of stitches. On a separate sheet, record the sample-number and details, such as how many rows have Colour A in the main yarn-feed and Colour B as the contrast colour, on which row the pattern card was locked, rewound, elongated, etc. My basic sample set was knitted in an oiled Shetland yarn. All the examples shown have been washed in a mild soap to remove the oil, allowing the knitting to 'bulk out' and become soft to the touch.

Using two contrasting colours

Pattern A (fig 18)
Sample 1 – the basic pattern
Cast on 40 stitches in Dark Grey yarn at Tension 9. Knit 6 rows plain knit.

Row Counter	Yarn feed A	Feed B	Pattern card action
000–004	Dark Grey (DG)	Cream (C)	Normal throughout
004–008	C	DG	
008–012	DG	C	
012–016	C	DG	
016–020	DG	C	
020–024	C	DG	
024–028	DG	C	
028–032	C	DG	
032–036	DG	C	
036–040	C	DG	
040–044	DG	C	
044–048	C	DG	
048–056	DG	C	
056–064	C	DG	
064–072	DG	C	
072–080	C	DG	
080–088	DG	C	
088–096	C	DG	

Row Counter	Yarn feed A	Feed B	Pattern card action
000–004	DG	C	Locked.
004–016	C	DG	Advance normally.
016–020	DG	C	Locked.
020–022	DG	–	Knit plain and reset needles on row 021.
022–068	DG	C	Elongate.
068–070	DG	–	Knit plain and reset needles on Row 069.
070–074	DG	C	Locked.
074–086	C	DG	Advance normally.
086–090	DG	C	Locked.
090–138	C	DG	Set card to Row 1 to begin this section.

Cast off at Row 138.

Knit 48 rows pattern, with foreground Dark Grey (feed A), background Cream (feed B).

This makes up one complete cycle of the pattern. Swap the foreground and background yarns over.

Knit 48 rows of pattern, and cast off. The card moves 1 position per row throughout.
Sample 2 – changing negative and positive colours
This sample experiments with changing negative and positive (background and pattern) colours regularly throughout the complete pattern sequence. I always find it easier to work from a chart for this type of knitting, hence the following. *Note that the number of rows in a group changes from 4 to 6, then to 8.*
Cast on 48 stitches in Dark Grey oiled Shetland, Tension 9.
Cast off at Row 096, after two complete repeats of the pattern.

Sample 3 – elongating the pattern
Most punchcard machines have the means to elongate a pattern by setting them so that the punchcard advances once only for every two passes of the knitting carriage. Do this working through Pattern A

Right **Fig 19.** *Pattern graph B.*

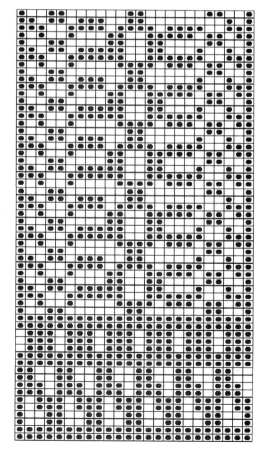

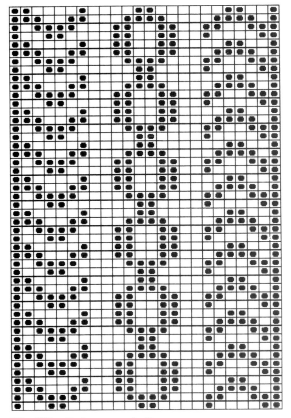

Fig 20. *Pattern graph C.*

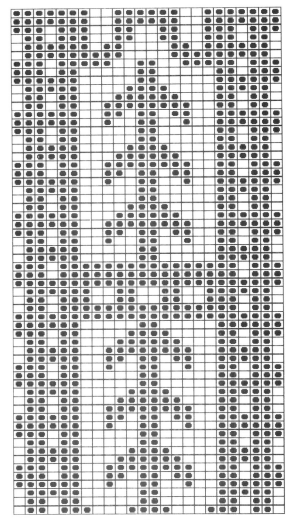

Fig 21. *Pattern graph D.*

punchcard to give you one elongated version of 96 rows in total.

Sample 4 – alternate locking and rotating of the punchcard
The card is alternatively locked on 4 rows, with Dark Grey in Feed A and Cream in Feed B, and rotated normally for 12 rows with Cream in the Feed A and Dark Grey in Feed B.

These 16 rows form the pattern, and are repeated four times (64 rows total).

Sample 5 – combining locked, elongated and rotated knitting
The pattern is locked, elongated, and knitted normally (rotated) in the following sequence. Work from the chart.

Pattern B (fig 19)
Test this card in much the same way as Pattern A, using the same yarns (Cream and Grey oiled Shetland). Tension is set at 9 throughout; knit across 40

stitches. Try working out a series of experiments based on samples 1–6.

Pattern C (fig 20)
Sample 6 – combining different card actions
Cast on 40 stitches using the Dark Grey oiled Shetland. Set Tension 9. Knit 6 rows of plain knitting.

Fig 22. *Pattern graph E.*

Fig 23. *Pattern graph F.*

Row Counter	Yarn feed A	Feed B	Pattern card action
000–002	C	–	Advance normally, plain knit.
002–010	C	DG	as above, patt. knit.
010–012	DG	–	as above, plain knit.
012–015	C	DG	as above, patt. knit.
015–017	DG	–	as above, plain knit.
017–058	C	DG	as above, patt. knit.
058–092	DG	C	Rewind card back to line 18; lock the card, knit 1 row to set the needles; release the card, set on elongate.
092–100	C	DG	Elongate.
100–128	C	DG	Advance normally.

Sample 7 – a variation

Cast on 40 stitches using Cream oiled Shetland. Use Tension 9.

Knit 6 rows plain knit. Follow the chart for Sample 6, but only as far as Row 058. Rows 058–060 are knitted in Dark Grey (Feed B). Reset the row counter to 000. Now follow the chart again for Sample 6 from 000–017. For rows 017–058 swap the yarns (Cream becomes the pattern colour, Dark Grey the background).

Patterns D, E and F (Figs 21, 22 and 23)

These samples have been knitted without any variations to give your imagination and creativity free rein.

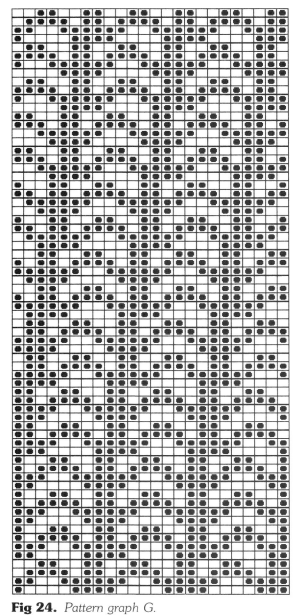

Fig 24. *Pattern graph G.*

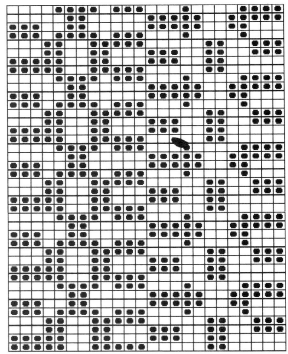

Fig 25. *Pattern graph H.*

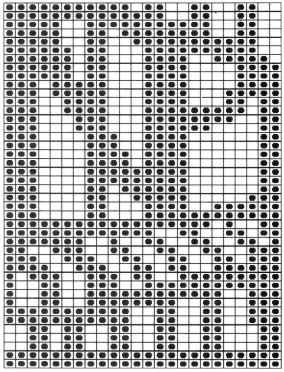

Fig 26. *Pattern graph J.*

Pattern G (fig 24)
All the samples in this group use the Dark Grey and Cream oiled Shetland, at Tension 9, and are 40 stitches wide.

The first two samples have the pattern-card advancing normally, switching main and contrasting yarns in feeds A and B. The next two samples use the elongate mechanism swapping main and contrast yarns every 8 rows.

Sample 8 – the basic pattern with single colour rows inserted

2 rows of plain knitting are inserted in the pattern after the first 8 rows, making 10 rows in all. This 10-row sequence is repeated nine times in total.

The card is locked prior to knitting the first plain row (009). The needles are reset on Row 010 for 2-colour knitting, and the carriage buttons are reset for patterned knitting prior to starting the next 10-row sequence.

In my sample, the main colour was Dark Grey, contrast yarn Cream.

Sample 9 – a variation, reversing feeds A and B

This sample develops Sample 8 further. The 10-row sequence is identical except that on every alternate repeat, the yarns are in reversed position for the pattern card section.

Row Counter	Yarn feed A	Feed B	Pattern card action
000–008	DG	C	Pattern card.
008–010	DG	–	Plain knit.
010–012	C	DG	Pattern card.
012–020	DG	–	Plain knit.

Pattern H (fig 25)

Here variations are shown using combinations of elongated pattern section and normal-length pattern.

Patterns J (fig 26) and K (fig 27)

These two cards can either be used consecutively to form one large pattern (in combination with sections of other pattern cards) or Pattern J can be used independently. They can also be used in combination with any of the other patterns in this group.

A compilation sample using Patterns A, B, J and K is illustrated in fig. 45. It is a more complex version derived from the starting point:

Sample 10 – combining patterns A, B, J and K

Yarns used:

Yeoman black Opium and Yeoman black Grisby, combined as a single end.

Yeoman white Elsa, Yeoman white Opium, combined as a single end.

The sample is knitted over 60 stitches, Tension 6 throughout.

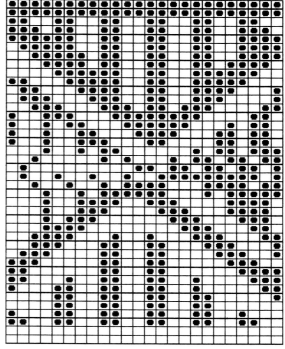

Fig 27. *Pattern graph K.*

Use White. Knit 5 rows plain knitting.

Insert Pattern A. Knit 1 row to set for pattern.

Using Black as main colour, White as contrast, knit 12 rows.

Change to Pattern K.

Lock on Row 1. Use White. Knit 4 rows plain knit, using the last row to set for patterned knit.

Release the pattern card to knit normal pattern-length.

Use White as main colour, Black as contrast.

Knit the complete pattern (42 rows).

Insert Pattern B.

Use Black. Knit 2 rows plain, using the second row to prepare for patterned knitting.

Release the card on normal pattern-length.

Use White as main colour, Black as contrast. Knit 8 rows.

Insert Pattern J. Use Black. Knit 2 rows, using the second row to prepare for patterned knit.

Release card on normal-length pattern.

Use White as main yarn, Black as contrast.

Knit one complete pattern repeat. Replace card with Pattern A.

Use White. Knit 2 rows. Second row prepares for patterned knit.

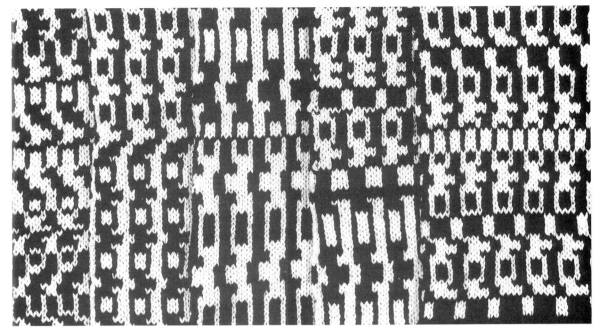

Above **Fig 28.** *Variations on Pattern A. Knitted samples 1 to 5; 2-colour patterned knit.*

Right **Fig 29.** *Pattern B. Sample knitted in a dark grey and cream Shetland yarn.*

Use Black as main yarn, White as contrast.
Knit 12 rows.
Use White. Knit 4 rows plain knit.
Cast off.

Increasing colour and textural awareness

The following series of samples features various qualities of yarn. Alternative balances of colour and tonal contrast are tried together with the introduction of additional colours. The latter are kept within the limited range already suggested, and include greeny-greys, blue-greys, neutral greys, off-whites, dark browns, beige, charcoal and cream.

Toward the end of this section I have included several small pattern units in graph form which are divisible into 24, giving you the chance to build up your own combinations of patterns, or to apply them to other repeat systems.

For instance if you own an electronic type of machine, designs using a far greater width than 24

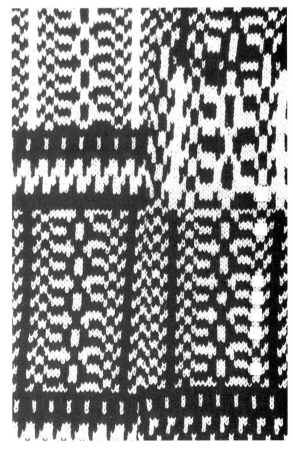

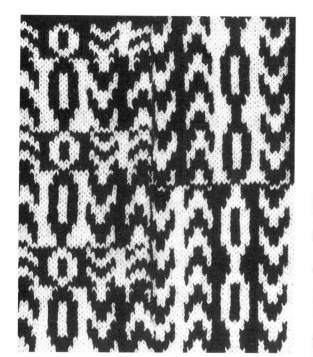

Fig 30. *Variations on Pattern C. Knit samples 6 and 7; two-colour patterned knit.*

stitches can be created. You can also introduce double-width and double-length patterns, mirroring, reversing, and offsetting patterns by altering the 1st needle position of subsequent rows of the same pattern. You can isolate small sections of a larger pattern and apply the same variations already mentioned – and this is all before any considerations of colour, yarn, and tension changes.

You could also try to combine a few of your own ideas, aiming eventually to move to a far more individual set of patterns.

This small group of six samples develops the 2-colour Grey and Cream sample by introducing one or two more distinct contrasts – a mid-grey and a light grey yarn.

All samples use 40 stitches at Tension 9 (see fig 35) and are based on Pattern G.

Fig 31. *Pattern D. Sample knitted in a dark grey and cream Shetland yarn.*

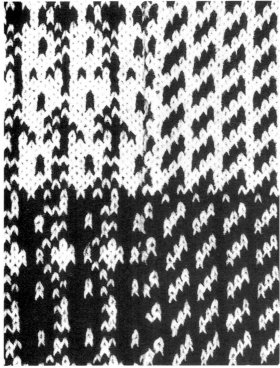

Fig 32. *Patterns E and F. Two-colour patterned knit. Cream and dark-grey Shetland yarn.*

Sample 11 – producing a striped pattern

Row counter	Yarn feed A	Feed B	Pattern card action
000–008	Dark Grey (DG)	Cream (C)	Card locked.
008–009	Mid-Grey (MG)	–	Plain knit.
009–010	MG	–	Plain knit, but use this row to set needles or pattern-drum for 2-colour knit.
010–018	DG	C	Release card.
018–019	MG	–	Lock card – plain knit.
019–020	MG	–	Plain knit (as 010 but leave card on lock).

These 20 rows form the repeat sequence. Knit 60 rows and cast off.

Fig 34. *Pattern H. Two-colour patterned knit. Variations of normal length and elongated patterns.*

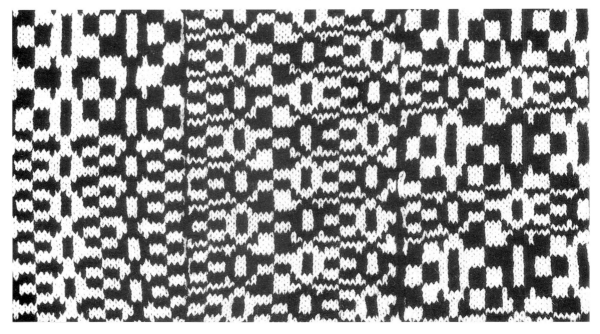

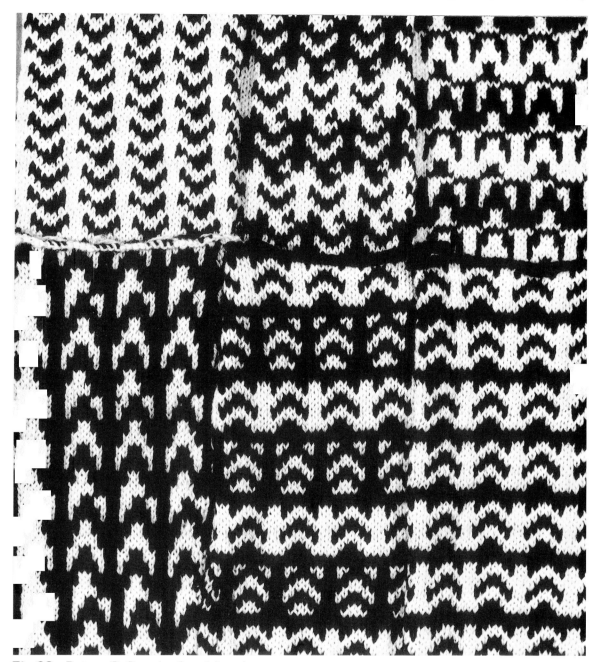

Fig 33. *Pattern G. Samples 8 and 9 and variations. Two-colour patterned knit.*

Try samples in which the number of rows in each band of patterned or plain knit is varied to produce thin and thick stripes.

Sample 12 – a variation
Bands of pattern in two different widths are knitted using the same basic format as the previous sample. The main pattern bands are 20 rows deep, and the striped bands 6 rows deep, divided by 2 rows of plain knitting in Mid Grey.

31

Sample 13 – a more complicated variation
Knit 6 rows in Cream.

Row Counter	Yarn feed A	Feed B	Pattern card action
000–006	Cream (C)	Dark Grey (DG)	Card locked.
006–007	Mid-Grey (MG)	–	Plain knit.
007–008	MG	–	Reset needles or pattern drum for 2-colour knit. Release card.
008–028	DG	C	Normal-length pattern.
028–029	MG	–	Plain knit.
029–030	MG	–	As 007–008 but leave card on lock.
030–038	C	DG	Card locked.
038–039	MG	–	Plain knit.
039–040	MG	–	As 007–008.
040–052	C	DG	Normal-length patt.
052–053	MG	–	Plain knit.
053–054	MG	–	As 029–030.
054–058	DG	C	Card locked.
058–059	MG	–	Plain knit.
059–060	MG	–	As 029–030.
060–068	C	DG	Card locked.
068–070	MG	–	Plain knit.

Cast off.

Sample 14 – reversing two of the colours
This sample is the same as Sample 13, except that the positions of mid-grey and cream are swapped.

Sample 15 – adding colours
Here, a lighter grey cotton is introduced alongside the mid-grey, dark-grey and cream yarns.

Row Counter	Yarn feed A	Feed B	Pattern card action
000–006	Light Grey (LG)	Dark Grey (DG)	Card locked.
006–008	Mid-Grey (MG)	–	Plain knit and reset.

Row Counter	Yarn feed A	Feed B	Pattern card action
008–028	Cream (C)	DG	Normal-length patt.
028–030	MG	–	Plain knit.
030–038	LG	DG	Card locked.
038–040	MG	–	Plain knit.
040–052	DG	C	Normal-length patt.
052–054	MG	–	Plain knit.
054–058	C	DG	Card locked.
058–060	MG	–	Plain knit.
060–068	DG	LG	Card locked.
068–070	MG	–	Plain knit.

Cast off.

Sample 16 – adding different patterns
I decided at this point in the experiment that although I was achieving variations and balances in tone, the

Fig 36. *Sample 16. Pattern cards B and G combined.*

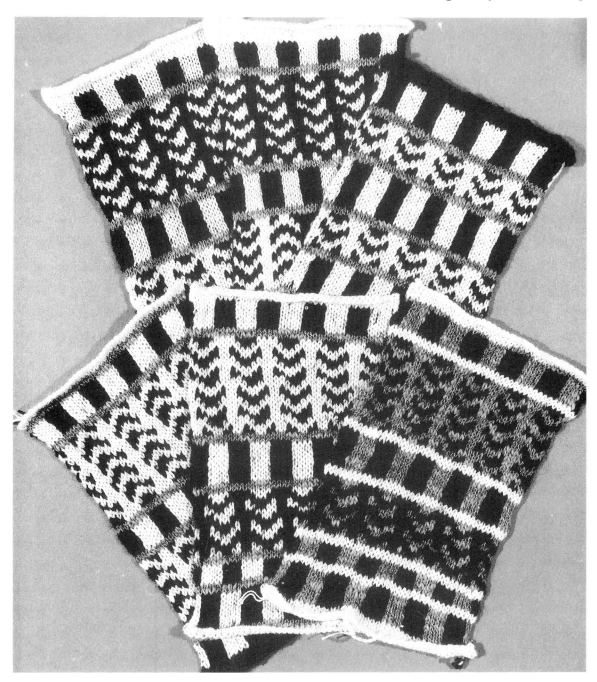

Fig 35. *Samples 11 to 15. A group of samples using alternative tonal balances based on Pattern G (see Fig 33). Cream and grey Shetland wool, mid-grey linen and cotton mix.*

pattern shapes were too similar. So I chose to insert a band of Pattern B to give the necessary contrast between the rounded shapes of this card and all the straight lines of Pattern G.

The differences were that rows 040–052 used Pattern B, and in order to include two repeats of the pattern, an additional 4 rows needed to be knitted for this section (040–056).

Fig 37. *Examples of knitting using a range of yarns to make solid and mixed colours.*

To follow the original directions (Sample 11), I reset the row-counter to 052 at the finish of this subsection. The only other alteration was at 054–058, where I replaced the cream yarn with a cotton/ linen mix in greeny-grey, adding one more element to the design.

Try a long version of this sample, with a rib or hem to complement the design. I envisage a man's Raglan sleeve sweater developing from this sample – the angular shape of the garment would fit in with the overall geometric qualities of the surface pattern.

Using many different yarns

Yet more colours and mixes of yarn are now introduced to ring the changes on the same design (see figs 37 and 38), and the last few samples use a much wider range of yarns, setting textured yarns against smooth and silky ones.

The samples are merely suggestions. Each pattern, with all the suggested combinations, is capable of generating many successful variations.

Fig 38. *Pattern K. Various mixes of yarns; two per swatch.*

Choose a sample that you have already worked which you especially like. If you have a good selection of small oddments of yarn saved from other projects, then now is the time to use them.

The emphasis for these samples has been placed on making changes to the pattern through textural contrasts, by reversing the foreground and background colours at differing points, and varying the amount of contrast between light and dark areas. (The colours listed refer to Yeoman Yarns catalogue – see list of stockists.)

Sample 17 (fig 39) – using four different yarns
The pattern is knitted using four qualities of yarn:

Black cotton (A)
Cream quality 67 (B)
Cord quality 69 (C)
Linen quality 68 (D)

Using Cream yarn (B), Pattern G and Tension 10, cast on 40 stitches over the centre of the needle-bed. Knit 6 rows. Set the row counter to 000.

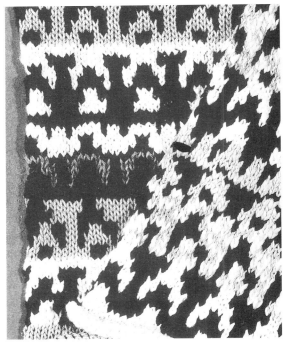

Fig 39. *Samples 17 (right) and 20 (left). Two-colour patterned knit using several combinations of contrasting textured yarns.*

Fig 40. *Samples 18 and 19. Identical arrangement of pattern in both samples, but altering the placings of the light and dark coloured yarns.*

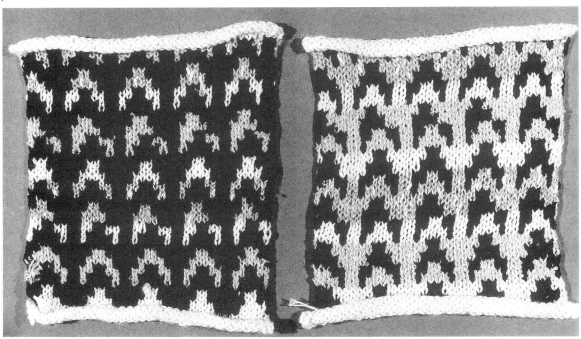

Row counter	Yarn feed A	Feed B	Pattern card action
000–010	Yarn B	Yarn A	Patt.card/elongate.
010–020	A	D	Patt.card/elongate.
020–025	C	A	Patt.card/elongate.
025–030	A	C	Patt.card/elongate.

Repeat this section as often as required.

Sample 18 (fig 40) – using four contrasting yarns knitted at Tension 8 over 40 stitches.
The yarns used are:

Black chenille (A)
White Jackie (B)
Silver Jackie (C)
Honey Jackie (D)

Knit 6 rows plain, and set for pattern knitting.

Row counter	Yarn feed A	Feed B	Pattern card action
000–010	B	A	Patt.card/elongate.
010–020	A	C	Patt.card/elongate.
020–025	D	A	Patt.card/elongate.
025–030	A	B	Patt.card/elongate.

These 30 rows form the repeat sequence.

Sample 19 (fig 40) – an alternative colouring
More textural interest has also been added. Knitted at Tension 8. The yarns used here are:

Black Cannel (A)
Silver Elsa and Silver Grigna combined (B)
Cream Husky (C)
Camel Poodle mixed with a 2-ply Beige Shetland (Jamieson & Smith) (D)

Fig 41. *Sample 21. Varying the tonal balance and introducing new textures.*

Row counter	Yarn feed A	Feed B	Pattern card action
000–010	B	A	Patt.card/elongate.
010–020	A	C	Patt.card/elongate.
020–025	D	A	Patt.card/elongate.
025–030	A	B	Patt.card/elongate.

Sample 20 (fig 39) – incorporating more plain knitting
Knit 40 stitches at Tension 10. The yarns used here are:

Black cotton/Viscose Flamme (A)
Cream quality 67 (B)
String Cannel (C)
Silver Jackie (D)

Row counter	Yarn feed A	Feed B	Pattern card action
000–010	B	A	Patt.card/elongate.
010–012	B	–	Lock card. Change to plain knit, but use 012 to reset needles or pattern drums.
012–022	A	C	Patt.card/elongate.
022–024	A	–	Lock card as 010–012.
024–029	D	A	Patt.card/elongate.
029–034	A	B	Patt.card/elongate.
034–036	A	–	Lock card as 010–012.

Repeat this sequence as many times as required. Try varying the number of rows of plain knit between the pattern sections.

Sample 21 (fig 41) – varying the tonal balance
Knit 40 stitches at Tension 10, with the card on Elongate. The main colour is continually changed, while the background yarn remains constant. Yarns used are:

Black chenille (A)
Beige Poodle and Shetland mix (2-ply) (B)
Cream Husky (C)
Grey mix (Silver Elsa and Silver Grigna) (D)

The main yarn changes for the example on the left are:

Row Counter	Yarn
000–004	C
004–012	B
012–016	C
016–024	D
024–028	C
028–036	B
036–040	C
040–048	D

Sample 22 (fig 42) – reversing the procedure
Use the same yarns as in Sample 21. This time the

Fig 42. *Sample 22. Background colour (black chenille) remains constant, foreground changes in tone and texture.*

main yarn remains constant (Black chenille) and the contrast yarns are changed at regular intervals. The contrast yarn changes are:

Row Counter	Yarn
000–004	C
004–012	B
012–016	C
016–024	D
024–028	C
028–036	B
036–040	C
040–048	D

Fig 43. *Samples 23 (right) and 24 (left). various formats and variations in the distribution of light, medium and dark tones alongside textural variations.*

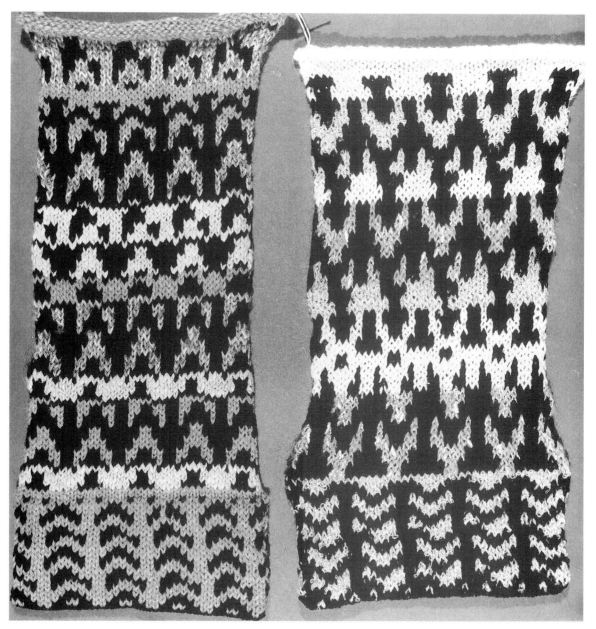

Sample 23 (fig 43) – distribution of colour and texture

This sample ends with a patterned hem, using Black cotton and Beige Poodle mixed with 2-ply Shetland, using Pattern G on normal length. Knit 20 rows in pattern, 2 plain-knit rows for the fold, and 20 more rows in pattern. Pick up stitches to make hem, then cast off.

Attach after the main sample has been knitted using:

Black cotton (A)
Beige Poodle/Shetland 2-ply (mixed) (B)
Cream Husky (C)
Grey (Silver Elsa/Silver Grigna mixed) (D)

Row counter	Yarn feed A	Feed B	Pattern card action
000–004	A	C	Patt.card/elongate.
004–016	B	A	Patt.card/elongate.
016–020	A	C	Patt.card/elongate.
020–032	D	A	Patt.card/elongate.
032–036	A	B	Patt.card/elongate.
036–042	C	A	Patt.card/elongate.
042–048	A	C	Patt.card/elongate.
048–060	D	A	Patt.card/elongate.

Cast off.

I decided to try a hem with this sample as I thought there was enough potential in it to make it the basis of a simple garment.

This gave me enough to work on to produce the three conclusive samples for this section, ready made for the next step in the design process – application to a particular garment shape, and finally a completed piece of knitwear.

I have chosen four compatible yarns for Sample 24 that would work successfully together in a garment such as a cardigan, or a man's sweater.

Sample 24 (fig 43) – a variation on Sample 23
Yarns as follows:
Beige Shetland 2-ply jumper-weight (A)
Country Birch (B)
Black Cannel (C)
Cord quality 69 (D)

Yarn A can be obtained from Jamieson & Smith, B, C and D from Yeoman Yarns (see Suppliers).

Once again, start with the hem. Cast on using waste yarn. Knit several rows, then set up for pattern knitting.

Row counter	Yarn feed A	Feed B	Pattern card action
000–020	C	A	Normal length, pattern card.
020–022	A	–	Plain knit. Set needles on 022 for next section of pattern-knit.
022–042	C	A	Normal length, pattern card.

Make a hem by hooking up Row 001 on to the corresponding needles (making 2 stitches on each needle). Knit 1 row to link the hem. Reset the row counter to 000.

Row counter	Yarn feed A	Feed B	Pattern card action
000–004	C	A	Patt.card/elongate.
004–016	A	C	Patt.card/elongate.
016–020	C	D	Patt.card/elongate.
020–032	B	C	Patt.card/elongate.
032–036	C	A	Patt.card/normal length.
036–042	D	C	Patt.card/normal length.
042–048	C	D	Patt.card/normal length.
048–060	B	C	Patt.card/normal length.
060–066	A	C	Patt.card/normal length.
066–068	A	–	Plain knit, and set needles on Row 068 for pattern-knit.
068–078	C	B	Patt.card/elongate.
078–080	D	–	Plain knit.
080–084	A	–	Plain knit.

Sample 25 (fig 44) – a suggested sweater pattern
A small sample showing a possible pattern for a sweater, which could combine with either of Samples 23 and 24 as the design for a cardigan. The yarn details of the sample are:

Cord quality 69 (A)
Black slub cotton (B)

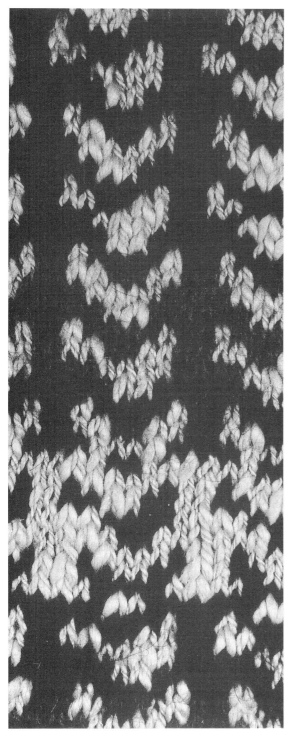

Fig 44. *Sample 25. Close-up showing contrast of texture. Idea for sweater to co-ordinate with Fig 43.*

Black Grisby and Charcoal Cigno (C)
Grey Jackie (D)

Knit 32 rows with Colour A as the main yarn, and Colours B, C and D changed at random to give a slightly shaded effect. Knit another 8 rows reversing the background colour for the foreground.

Change back to the original set-up, and knit another 12 rows of pattern with Colour A as the main yarn. A contrasting band of pattern interrupts the main body of knitting.

If you want to try your own variations, decide where you want to bring in the new colour, count up the number of rows on the card to this point, and make a note of where the exchange of colours will take place.

Either mark the card in pencil or keep a notebook by your side. This is always useful for jotting down alternative ideas to be tried at a later date. It may be that a certain section would look better if the main and contrasting yarns were exchanged, or perhaps you decide you would like to try more emphasis on one of the colours by knitting more rows in that colour.

Try introducing just one or two rows of the new colour as a plain stripe. A new lighter tone may give a highlighted area of pattern, perhaps in contrast with the darker colour, and in a proportionally small area relative to the sample as a whole. Or make changes by introducing mixes of yarn to replace some of the solid colours.

A note of caution here; do not try to put too many new ideas and changes down in one sample. The result is most likely to be visual mayhem, and potentially good ideas will be lost in the confusion and clutter.

I feel it is better to produce several samples, each one working out one particular idea. Keep a good written record, taking in the number of rows, position of yarn, colour changes, pattern card changes, where plain-knit rows have been introduced, elongated or normal length, and any other details you consider necessary.

When you have produced several such samples, you may decide that an area of one sample could work quite well with part of another sample. Work back from the original notes and rewrite a new set of instructions, then knit up the new sample. This can be an ongoing and fascinating process, revealing many new design ideas *en route*.

Perhaps you decide that you like the first 30 rows of a certain sample. Try repeating these rows by knitting to row 030, winding the card back to the beginning, and knitting the sequence again. A new card could eventually be made, taking in all the changes.

If you are working on an electronic machine, knit a particular sequence through one repeat. Re-program a new first-needle position to offset the next repeat sequence. This can be repeated as many times as desired. To produce a similar effect on a punchcard model of machine, a complete card would have to be made, with each variation in place.

Fig 45. *Sample 26. A composite design.*

Larger-scale designs

The final samples of this chapter look at ways of achieving a much larger-scale design using a greater variety of yarns – perhaps for a boldly patterned man's sweater, a jacket, or a long coat.

Sample 26 (fig 45) – combining four patterns
Patterns A, B, J and K are used.

Cast on 60 stitches using Yeoman's Country Birch (referred to as Tweed yarn). Knit 6 rows of plain knitting.
Knit 2 rows plain in Black Slub (Yeoman No 65).
Insert Pattern A. Lock on Row 1. Knit 2 rows in Cream, using the second row to set the needles/pattern drum for pattern knitting.
Release card. Knit 12 rows with Black in the main feed, White as the contrast colour.
Knit 2 rows Cream (plain knit).
Knit 2 rows Black (plain knit).
Knit 2 rows Cream (plain knit).
Insert Pattern K, and lock on Row 1. Knit 4 plain rows in Tweed yarn, using Row 4 to set the needles/pattern drums.
With 'String' cotton in the main feed, Black as the contrast, knit 42 rows of pattern.
Insert Pattern B. Lock on Row 1. Knit 2 rows in Black, using Row 2 to set the needles/pattern drums.
Main colour White, contrast Black. Knit in pattern for 8 rows. Insert Pattern J.
Use Black. Do 2 rows plain knit, use Row 2 to set the needles/pattern drums.
Knit 22 rows in pattern (the complete pattern).
Knit 4 rows plain knit in Tweed yarn.
Use White. Knit 2 rows plain knit.
Use Black. Knit 2 rows plain knit.
Insert Pattern A. Knit 2 rows plain knit in White, using Row 2 to set the needles/pattern drums.
Black as main yarn, White as contrast. Knit 12 rows pattern.
Use White. Knit 2 rows plain.
Use Black. Knit 2 rows plain.
Use Tweed. Knit 6 rows plain.
Cast off.

Sample 27 (fig 46) – using more textured yarns
Use Tension 10 over 60 stitches.
This sample follows exactly the same format, but replaces some of the yarns with more textured yarn. The White slub cotton becomes Cream chenille, and for Black, the cotton is exchanged for a Boucle mix.

Fig 46. *Sample 27. A composite design. Format as Fig 45 with a variation in use of yarns.*

The String-coloured cotton is replaced with a slub cotton.

Sample 28 (fig 47) – other pattern combinations
A sample using a mixture of pattern cards. The hem is Pattern G, while the main section of the knitting is Pattern J with bands of Pattern B.
 Cast on 40 stitches at Tension 8.
Band 1 4 rows Grey acrylic (Bramwell Yarns).
   2 rows Brown/Grey wool.
Band 2 Pattern B. Main colour Black Butterfly (Yeoman). Contrast colour Grey/Yellow mix. Knit the pattern, 4 rows card on lock, 8 rows normal length, and finally 4 rows on lock.

Fig 47. *Sample 28. Composite design to co-ordinate with either Fig 45 or Fig 46.*

Fig 48. *Close-up of fitted sweater knitted from Pattern A, in a slub cotton, wool and cotton mix, wool and linen mix, and 2-ply jumper weight Shetland wool.*

Band 3 2 rows Grey/Brown wool.
4 rows Grey acrylic.

Band 4 Pattern J. 40 rows. The main yarn is a Boucle mix in Beige. Contrast yarn Grey acrylic.

Band 5 Knit 1 row Grey/Brown wool, 1 row Grey/ Yellow mix. Now knit 8 rows Pattern B, with the main yarn the Grey/Yellow mix, the contrast yarn Yeoman's Butterfly.

Band 6 As Band 4, but with the pattern card turned upside down (but still facing the same way – ie a plane rotation rather than flipped over). Knit 40 rows.

Band 7 Knit 2 rows Brown/Grey wool.
Knit 2 rows Grey/Yellow mix.

Band 8 Pattern B. Knit 8 rows with main yarn Grey/ Yellow mix, contrast Black Butterfly.

Band 9 Knit 2 rows plain in Grey/Yellow. Knit 4 rows plain Grey acrylic.
Knit several rows in White, then cast off.

A hem is knitted using Pattern G on normal-length. This is sewn carefully on to the end of the main sample to indicate how a hem would look on a finished garment.

Once you have reached this stage, you should have completed enough sampling to have ideas that can be carried through to a finished garment (see fig 48).

If you are not used to designing your own garment shapes, choose a tried and tested pattern. Trace out or draw the shape for your charting device. Knit the appropriate type of tension square for your system. Measure off rows and stitches in order that the right stitch-ruler is chosen, and that the regulators for measuring the amount of rows are correctly set.

If, however, you do not own a charting device, measure 1cm in terms of rows and stitches, and apply this information to, for example, a simple T-shape pattern. For example if 1cm (0.39 in) equals 5 rows then 10cm (3.9 in) will need 10×5 rows, equalling 50 rows in total.

You will now be well on the way to producing your own individually designed knitting. Chapter 3 describes methods whereby you can design your own patterns for the punchcard from scratch, or make alterations to existing patterns.

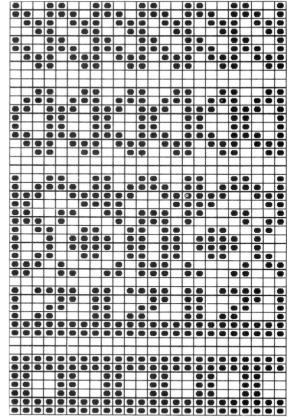

Fig 49. *Graph showing a collection of small related patterns for use with the main pattern-set.*

CHAPTER 2
Double-bed Jacquard knitting

Double-bed Jacquard knitting is a technique which produces a two-colour-in-a-row patterned fabric which is quite different in quality to that produced by the single-bed method.

Generally speaking a firmer and more solid structure results but with some elasticity, unlike the two-colour stranded knitting produced on one bed of needles. The most obvious difference between a single-bed two colour knit and a double-bed Jacquard knit is the lack of 'floats' stranded across the back of the knitting.

The second major difference is the ability to produce a more varied range of designs. Patterns no longer need to be restricted to small areas of, for example, 8 stitches in width as a maximum. Instead, the total 24 stitches on a card, the full width of the electric sheet of 60 stitches (which can be doubled to 120 stitches) or, in some cases on the new generation of electronics, the full width of the needle-bed can be utilized in a shape if required. There are no dangling floats to snare jewellery and tangle on buttons when the garment is worn (see fig 50).

A third difference becomes apparent when experimenting with surface patterns. Double-bed Jacquard is generally worked on a strict rotation of four-row sequences so it is less easy to stop and restart the pattern card to produce new images. This is something of a drawback, although not a serious one. I have therefore suggested samples that vary yarns, weights, tension and colour changes and so on, rather than alterations to the pattern itself. Some experimentation in pattern alteration while knitting can be undertaken, but must be done with care.

Fig 50. *Pattern graph for a large-scale double-bed Jacquard motif (electronic machines).*

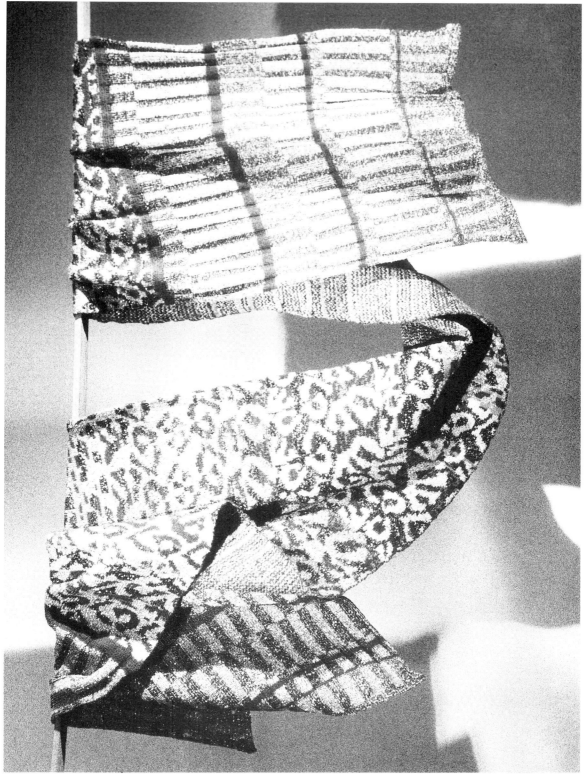

Fig 51. *Evening wrap in fine cottons, wools, and industrial weight lurex.
Uses double-bed Jacquard and 2-colour ribbing.*

47

The technique used to be regarded as an industrial method giving a mass-produced look. However the general improvements made to the Jacquard facilities on the domestic machines, and a more readily available supply of fine industrial-weight yarns, has made it possible to knit a successful double-bed Jacquard across a range of gauges.

Varying combinations of yarn types, choice of tensions, and size of pattern repeat give the adventurous knitter much scope in this area.

I have found Jacquard to be an excellent vehicle for producing rich, lush fabrics, often involving several fine strands of yarn plied together to make one end, to knit either the background or the pattern areas or both.

Subtle tonal and colour changes can be made by exchanging maybe one or two of the strands within the bunch. I quite often incorporate very fine strands of industrial-weight Lurex, or perhaps knit on a very fine gauge with luxury yarns (Celandine Yarns stock a good collection of qualities for just this purpose). This type of knitting, particularly involving many colour and yarn changes, could not be readily produced by a factory at economic rates. It is possible to produce beautiful one-offs, or variations on a pattern theme, taking double-bed Jacquard into the realms of the craft knitter (see figs 51, 52, 54).

Take as inspiration some of the fine brocade look of the seventeenth-century Florentine jackets housed in the Victoria and Albert Museum, and other European and American collections. They are knitted in silk, in two colours, sometimes with the purl stitches right-side-facing enhancing the brocaded look.

These jackets, and waistcoats of similar style, were

Fig 52. *Detail from Fig 51.*

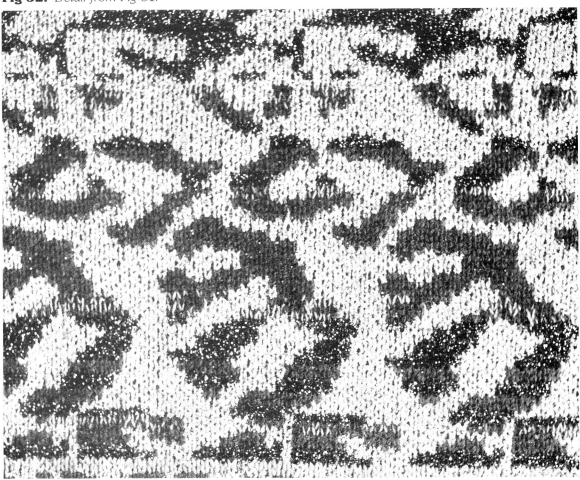

constructed as separate panels of knitted fabric and then sewn together (a technique which could be emulated with areas of Jacquard combined with areas of ribbing). It is thought that they were produced in Italy, or alternatively in England, by framework knitters of that period. At present their history is not altogether clear.

The patterned sections of these jackets reveal floats of yarn stranded across the back as in single-bed knitting, but there is no reason why double-bed methods cannot be used to produce hand-made luxury-type fabrics in a fine gauge, using ribbing to produce shaped sections.

If you have access to a machine such as the Pfaff

Fig 53. *Pattern graph. 24-stitch repeat, for Fig 51.*

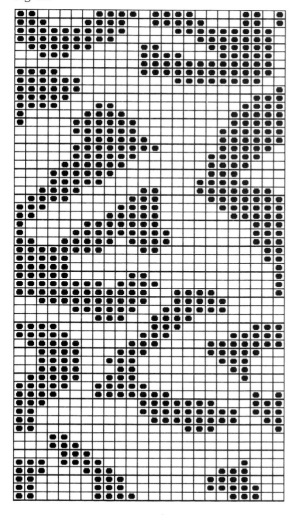

Electronic, many unusual combinations of plain and purl stitches can be worked together to produce raised patterned fabrics. The needle selection on the main bed of other types of machine can be altered, allowing the purl stitches to surface in certain areas. This method of working will be discussed in the sampling section.

Double-bed Jacquard knitting cannot be as easily moulded to shape when worn as can a knit structure with more elasticity, such as plain-knit intarsia, or non-patterned ribbing. However, on the plus side the nature of Jacquard knitting lends itself to cut-and-sew methods more readily than any other machine-knit method, with the exception, perhaps, of certain types of knit-weave.

A firm, dense knit is less likely to unravel after cutting the fabric, and can with care be sewn on an ordinary domestic sewing-machine, using a stretch stitch. This is a very useful feature, since shaping, especially increasing, is not an easy task on most domestic machines. Potential also exists for embroidery and appliqué additions to the knitting.

Method of production

Jacquard is, as already stated, a two-colour-in-a-row method of producing patterned knitting using the full needle Rib setting on a suitably linked double-bed machine. A punch card or an electronic patterning device determines the needle selection on the main bed. It is here that the actual design is produced. The ribber knits in the yarn that would normally produce a float on a single-bed knitted piece, and a double fabric is produced.

In order to understand the structure of Jacquard and be able to design for it, it is necessary to take a closer look at the method by which it is produced. This should help to give you the confidence either to adapt existing single-bed designs, or to work a new idea from scratch.

The first factor to consider is that the background and foreground colours are knitted on *separate rows*, unlike the single-bed method where both colours are knitted in on the same row. Hence it takes *four* movements of the carriage to produce *two* complete rows using this method.

To explain further, on most domestic machines the sequence is as follows:-

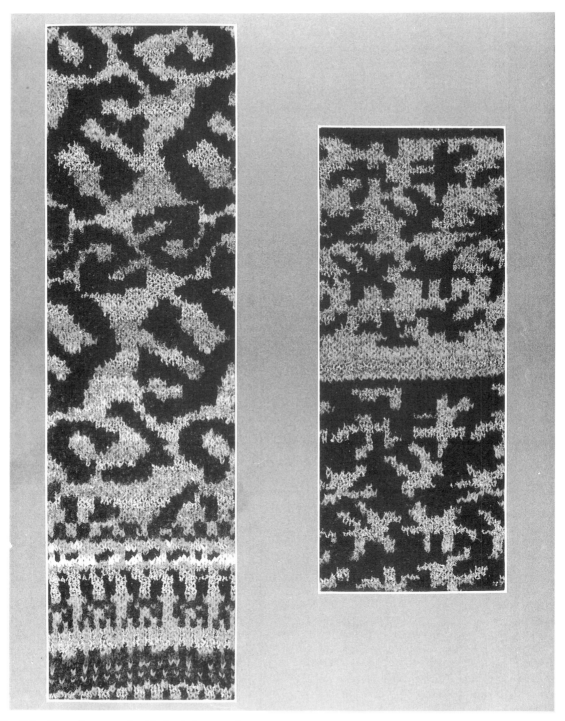

Fig 54. *Coordinating double-bed Jacquard patterns, designed to be used together as contrasting panels in an evening jacket. Fine wools, lurex, mohair mixes and chenille.*

Row 1 On the main bed, needles are selected for the background colour and knitted in Colour A, while the needles relating to the foreground colour of that particular row are slipped. The needles on the ribber knit on either every needle, or every alternate needle, on every row.

Row 2 On the main bed the needles are selected for the foreground colour of the previous row, and are knitted with Colour B. The needles selected on the previous row are slipped. The ribber continues as above (Row 1).

Row 3 On the main bed, the needles for the foreground of the next row are selected and knitted in Colour B, while the stitches relating to the background colour for this row are slipped. The ribber continues as before.

Row 4 On the main bed the needles for the background colour *for the previous row* are selected and knitted in Colour A. The stitches relating to the foreground are slipped. The ribber continues as before.

This completes the four row sequence, which is repeated throughout.
To sum up:

* Row 1 of the sequence knits the background stitches to row 2.
* Row 2 knits the foreground stitches to Row 1.
* Row 3 knits the foreground stitches to Row 4.
* Row 4 completes Row 3 by knitting the background colour.

If you substitute the words 'positive' for foreground, and 'negative' for background, a simple chart can be compiled:

Row 1 = a negative row (Colour A)
Row 2 = a positive row (Colour B)
Row 3 = a positive row (Colour B)
Row 4 = a negative row (Colour A)
Now repeat the sequence.

Rows 1 and 2 work together, as do rows 3 and 4. Colour A is knitted for two consecutive rows before an exchange of colour takes place. Colour B is then knitted for a further two rows. This is for a practical reason as the colours not being knitted are held in a colour changer on one side of the machine, allowing colours to be switched without having to be broken off and rethreaded.

The device also prevents loose ends of yarn

appearing on the edge of the fabric (unless one of the yarns in the changer is swapped for a fresh one) since normally the yarn changing always takes place on the same side of the machine.

The colour changer or striper usually allows for at least four colours to be set up at any one time. Once all the details are mastered, the actual knitting goes relatively quickly, particularly if only four colours are used in the one piece of knitting.

While considering the method of production using Jacquard, a look at the role of the ribber is essential. Depending on the make and model of machine that you own, either (a) a striper-type or (b) a birdseye Jacquard will be produced. The main difference

Fig 55. *Pattern graph for large design in fig 54.*

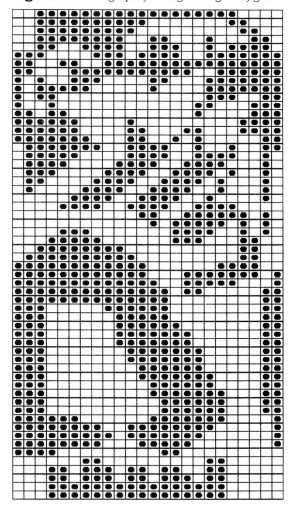

51

between (a) and (b) is that in the former type, all needles in working position on the ribber-bed knit on every row, producing a very solid Jacquard.

A disadvantage with this method appears when thicker yarns are used. A rather unwieldly type of fabric results even if the yarns knit off successfully. The birdseye Jacquard allows only alternate needles to knit on the rib-bed on alternate rows. This produces a lighter weight of fabric, but also provides the benefit of allowing thicker yarns to be knitted if required.

As an example, the Brother ribber model 881, which goes with the popular 24-stitch repeat main-bed machines and the Electronic, works over a two-row sequence. The main machine as always knits the pattern, while the ribber setting knits alternate stitches, slipping the remainder on one row.

On the second row of the sequence the slipped stitches of Row 1 knit, and the knitted stitches slip. This will only work over an even number of stitches, and can cause problems with shaping if the mechanics involved in knitting birdseye are not understood.

The following explanation and diagrams elaborate on this, looking at the ribber-bed only.

Example 1

Colour A and Colour B are used.

The carriage is on the left-hand side. Colour A to knit. All the existing stitches are in Colour B.

The needle setting is over an even number of stitches, *e.g.* 10.

Knit a row from left to right using Colour A. Alternate needles knit in Colour A.

Knit from right to left using Colour A again. The needles still holding stitches in Colour B now knit, leaving all the needles holding Colour A.

Please note that on this model of machine, the first needle to knit on the ribber is always the second needle in from the end.

Colour	Carriage direction	Sequence
A	→	B*ABABABAB*A
A	←	*AAAAAAAAAA*
B	→	A*B*A*B*A*B*A*B*A*B*
B	←	*BBBBBBBBBB*

(The italic letters (eg A or B) are those stitches which are knitted on that particular row.)

It is not important whether the needle setting commences with an odd or even number on the needle-bed, but it *is* important to have an even number of stitches on the ribber.

Try carefully repeating the above sequence with an odd number of stitches. The result is catastrophic. The same alternate needles knit throughout, always slipping the same stitches and the knitting will immediately bunch up and tangle.

Nine stitches are used instead of ten for this example, which again uses Colour A and Colour B.

Colour	Carriage direction	Sequence
A	→	B*ABABABAB*
A	←	B*ABABABAB*
B	→	B*ABABABAB*
B	←	B*ABABABAB*

The reason for this is that the ribber selection always chooses the second stitch in to knit at the beginning of any one row.

Understanding the Jacquard punchcard

A separate row of punching is required for the positive (foreground stitches) and the negative (background stitches) of the pattern. This is the reason why Jacquard cards are double the length of a similar single-bed pattern card.

Each single full row of knitting requires the punching of two rows on the punch-card. Almost any standard 24-stitch repeat pattern can be converted to Jacquard, as long as it contains an even number of rows (since there is a 4-row sequence which must be completed). You could perhaps consider using one of the designs produced while working on single-bed patterns.

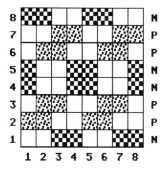

P = Positive rows
N = Negative rows
⬛ = Colour A
▨ = Colour B

Fig 56. *Diagram indicating negative and positive rows necessary when designing double-bed Jacquard punchcards.*

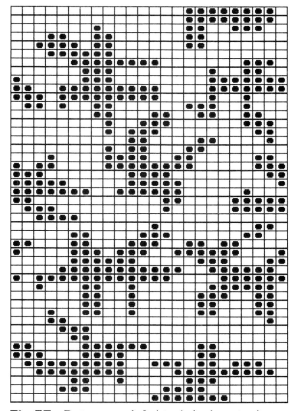

Fig 57. *Pattern graph L (single-bed version).*

Converting a standard single-bed card to Jacquard

Select a design. Count the number of rows involved. Multiply this figure by two, then add four extra rows to allow for the overlap of the punch-card where the two ends are joined together. My example is Pattern L (fig 57), which is converted to Jacquard in Pattern M (fig 58).

If you find that a single length of card is not long enough (this frequently happens) then simply clip on another section. I find that in the long run, a roll of punch-card material is more economical than packs of separate cards.

Take the blank punch-card material and, using a softish pencil, mark out all the positive rows as follows.

Beginning on line 2, mark out the first row of the design.

On line 3 mark out the second row of the design.

Now leave 2 complete rows blank. These will be filled in later.

Continue in this way until the whole design has been transferred to the card. A single unpunched row

must be left between the last pattern row and the two rows marked out for the overlap.

The negative (or background) rows can now be marked out for punching. These are plotted on the card in the rows between the already marked rows.

Start at the bottom of the card with the first single unmarked row. On this row, mark out all the holes corresponding to the holes which are *not* marked on the above row (i.e. the first positive row.)

Move on to the next 2 blank rows. On the first of these, mark out all the spaces adjacent to those *not* marked on the positive row below. For the other blank row, mark out all the spaces next to those *not* marked in the row above.

Continue in this way until all the blank rows have been completed. Note that there is only a single negative row following the final two positive rows. This single row pairs with the first single negative row at the beginning of the card, and is the negative, or background, row for the final positive row on the card.

Leave 2 extra blank rows for overlap.

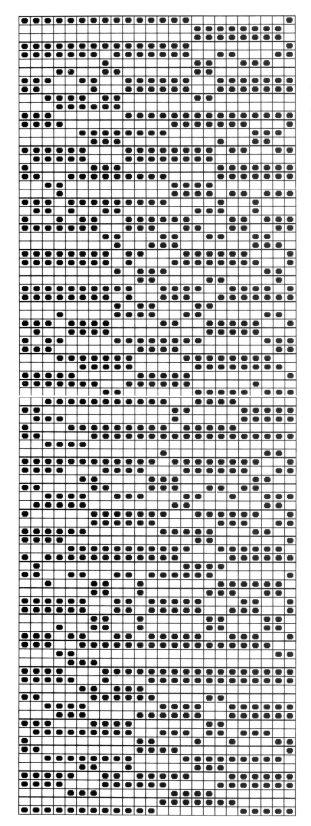

Left **Fig 58.** *Pattern graph M (double-bed version of Fig 57).*

Brother machines

The electronic machine will convert the single-bed pattern into Jacquard if the appropriate switches are used. The pattern is then read automatically to work out negative and positive rows. You should check with the individual machine's instruction manual regarding such options as double width or double length and so on (see figs 59–61).

Equipment required to produce double-bed Jacquard

In order to knit double-bed Jacquard two beds of needles are required. These comprise a main bed with either punch card or electronic patterning facilities, and a suitable ribber.

Individual companies will be able to give detailed information concerning the compatibility of various models, and also the type of Jacquard that each combination can produce.

You will also need a striper or colour-changer, plus a four-way tensioning device and some ribber weights – generally the more the better – and combs, if your model requires them.

You should collect a supply of suitable yarns. I suggest you try to get the best quality yarns you can afford (within reason.) Cheap, rough yarns will strain and snap easily under the stresses they experience working on a double-bed machine, especially on full-needle rib under tension. If you are learning a new technique, it is important that you are able to determine which of the inevitable problems that arise are due to your own inexperience, rather than failure of equipment or materials. Good quality yarn and a clean, well looked-after machine will make life a lot easier in this respect.

A list of machines and ribbers made by various companies which are suitable for Jacquard knitting is contained in the appendix.

Top right **Fig 59.** *Electronic Jacquard. Sweater-weight wools in solid and flecked shades from Mary-a-Mickle.*

Bottom right **Fig 60.** *Variations in scale of pattern developed from Fig 59.*

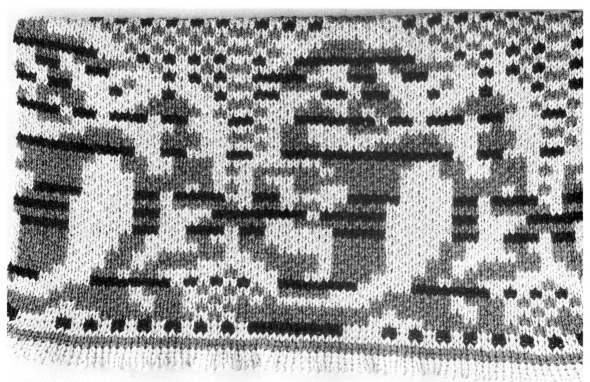

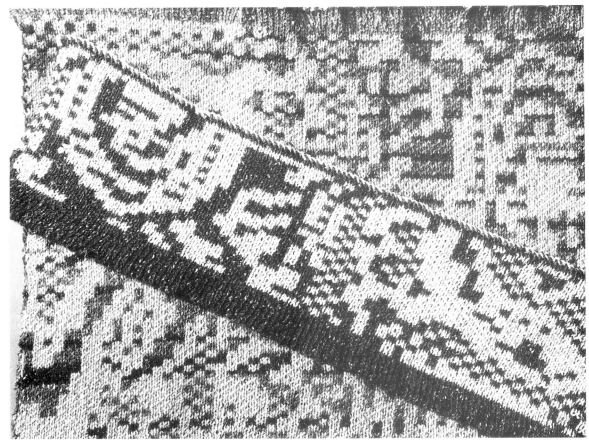

Fig 61. *More variations in scale of pattern development from Fig 59.*

The different types of Jacquard fabrics

Jacquard technique allows the production of fairly exotic and luxurious knitted fabrics, combining flat pattern with subtle changes of texture, and permitting a certain amount of manipulation and experimentation with the surface.

The Jacquard method can also be employed to produce rugged fabrics which can then be used to make hardwearing and easily laundered knitwear for leisure and sports use, children's wear, and warm winter clothing.

The results may be less spectacular than when the method is applied to more decorative ends, but the garments produced are warm, practical and functional. You can emphasize changes of colour rather than rich textural contrasts in fancy 'dry-clean only' fibres.

Prior to experimenting, always check that your machine is in tip-top condition, particularly the needles. Bent needles are especially troublesome when working double-bed methods, notably at low tensions.

Using exotic and unusual fibres

In this section I have tried to work the double-bed Jacquard method through a variety of exotic and luxurious yarns. The resulting fabric retains a firmness, yet is light weight to handle. Single-bed patterned knitting on such low tensions is less durable in wear; the fine floats could more easily snag and break.

I have tried to keep each of the first few samples of this section to four yarns only, since I am aware of the expense which can be incurred in purchasing a wider range of types or colours. However, Celandine do produce their luxury yarns in small units making it possible to extend your range.

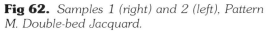

Fig 62. *Samples 1 (right) and 2 (left), Pattern M. Double-bed Jacquard.*

Sample 1 (fig 62) – developing the pattern
A series of samples has been knitted from the same Pattern (M), developing the pattern by varying colour, yarn type, and tension (see fig 62).

The first sample is worked at Tension 4/4 over 41 stitches on the main bed and 40 stitches on the ribber, using a birdseye type Jacquard. If you use a striper-type Jacquard you may need to loosen the tension to make up for the fact that all needles on the ribber are knitting on every row. Tension 4/4 may produce a knit that is too solid and tight.

The following yarns were used (all by Celandine):

Mink and lambswool mix 'Karen' Shade No 1 (A)
Mink and lambswool mix 'Karen' Shade No 6 (B)
Silk/cotton/acrylic mix 'Sienna' Shade No 4 (Brick) (C)
Silk/cotton/acrylic mix 'Sienna' Shade No 1 (Cream) (D)

The pattern is knitted in a 20 row sequence to be repeated as many times as required (see chart). Rows 000–001 are in the negative or background colour (cream), as are all the other background rows. Chart for 20 row sequence:

Row Counter	Colour
000–002	D
002–004	C
004–006	D
006–008	B
008–010	D
010–012	A
012–014	D
014–016	B
016–018	D
018–020	C

Sample 2 (fig 62) – a variation
Three colours only are used in this sample. A Grey background colour contrasting with two foreground colours of Cream and Brick silk – the Cream being the most dominant colour and the Brick being used in much smaller proportions.

The colour sequence is as follows:

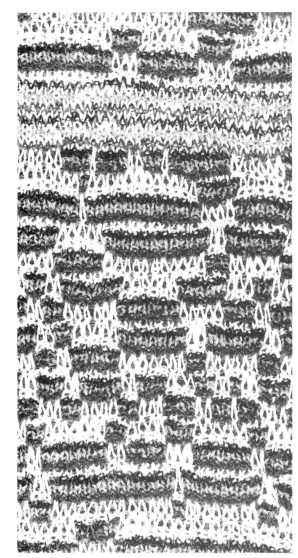

Fig 63. *Pattern M. Lightweight double-bed Jacquard ripple-effect fabric.*

Row Counter	Colour
000–002	Grey
002–004	Cream
004–006	Grey
006–008	Brick
008–010	Grey
010–012	Cream

The tension was dropped to 3/3 for this sample – the result being a lightweight delicate fabric.

Perhaps it is worth considering here the limitations imposed by fine-gauge jacquard. The limitations are mainly in the width of any one complete piece of knitting. A rough measurement of Sample 62 provides a gauge of 40 stitches = 10cm (3.9 in), which means that 200 needles (the full bed) would produce a width of around 50cm (19.5 in). If the tension was even lower – say 1/1 or 2/2 – less width would be achieved.

If this is noted at the start of any project, the garment or piece can be designed in sections, and this necessary procedure can be incorporated in the design of the piece. It would be possible to include inserts of, for example, full needle ribbing or other types of rib. Alternatively several patterned panels could be linked together in an imaginative way.

Sample 3 (figs 63 and 64) – creating a ripple effect
With this sample I experimented by setting the needles for the pattern, but the card remained locked at the same position for N rows.

The same needles knitted on each of the N rows, while the other needles (in normal working position) were constantly slipped, producing a ripple effect from the build-up up of rows knitting off the patterning needles. Between each section of ripples, rows of plain, full-needle rib were knitted, the carriage always being returned to the left-hand end of the needle-bed prior to commencing the next section.

Allow the card to move on by one position to choose different needles for the ripple rows.

The ripple effect works most successfully with fine yarns, as it is possible to build up a greater number of rows on the knitting stitches than if a more heavyweight yarn were used. In addition, fine yarns mean that a textured surface can be achieved with less weight and bulk.

It is important to be aware that the technique can distort the side edges of the knitting, and this fact must be taken into account at the design stage.

Fig 64. *Sample 3, Pattern M. Double-bed Jacquard.*

You should now be in a position to attempt a series of experiments from this sample by varying the number of rows in the pattern sections with respect to the ripple section, or by altering the colour change sequence.

The number of slipped rows can be varied within the limitation of the yarn thickness, as can the number of rows knitted on full-needle rib.

I think that the back of the knitting is of equal interest, and I can see possibilities of using the ripple surface (back) in conjunction with a Jacquard patterned section knitted in the usual way (see fig 64).

To recap:
Variations involve:
The number of rows knitted in any single section.
The order of the colour changes.
The introduction of bands of other stitch patterns.
Altering the tension.

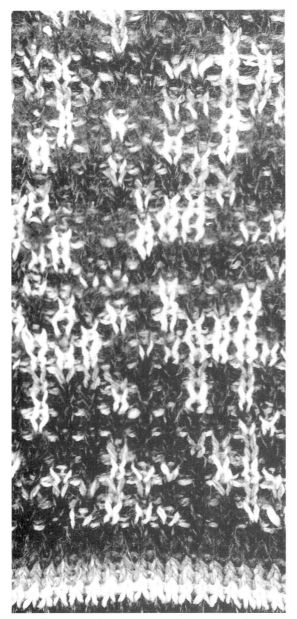

Fig 65. *Sample 4, Pattern M. Close-up showing alternative main-bed needle settings.*

Sample 4 (fig 65) – using a different needle-setting
This Jacquard uses a different needle-setting from all previous samples. Yarns used are Cream and Brick quality Sienna (A and B), Dark Purple quality Dawn (C), and Grey Suri Alpaca/Lambswool (D) – all from Celandine.

Cast on for a full-needle rib (41 stitches main bed, 40 on ribber). Set the tension to 3/3.

Knit 2 rows of each colour after the selvedge, ending with the carriage on the left.

Working from right to left on the main needle-bed, transfer every other needle to the next adjacent needle, pushing the empty needle into non-working position (NWP).

Knit the background in Grey and Dark Purple; use Cream and Brick for the pattern.

O = non-working position (NWP)
X = working position (WP)
Set the lever to half-pitch.

X O X O X O X O X O X
  X X X X X X X X X X

In this sample the pattern becomes less sharp as the stitches knitted on the ribber show through the gaps where the main-bed needles have been placed into NWP. This technique can work equally well with a striper Jacquard or a birdseye type, but will give a different effect.

Sample 5 (fig 66) – a variation
As sample 4, but with the following setting, and knitted at Tension 2/2.

X X O X X O X X O X X
  X X X X X X X X X X X
(note half-pitch)

For this sample the background is knitted in Colours C and A, while the design is knitted in Colours D and B at random.

You will notice that a more substantial fabric is produced, which still retains a ridge and shadow effect, and acts more like a full-needle rib Jacquard.

Sample 6 (fig 67)
Use tension 6/6 with 41 stitches on the main bed, and 40 on the ribber to produce a thicker luxury fabric more suited to outwear.

The background of section 1 (bottom) is knitted in Dark Brown alpaca; the design in White alpaca, Grey mink/lambswool mix, and Muted Pink acrylic/wool/alpaca mix. The pattern colours are changed at random, but the background remains constant.

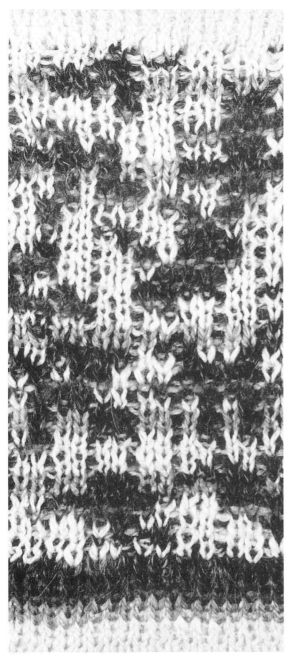

Fig 66. *Sample 5. Variation on Fig 65.*

Fig 67. *Sample 6, Pattern M. Double-bed Jacquard.*

Section 2 is knitted with Cream, Grey and Light Brown alpaca for the background, and Dark Brown alpaca for the actual design. The knitting can be brushed up with a teasel-brush to produce a luxurious hairy fabric.

The alpaca used in these samples can be obtained from Many-a-Mickle (see list of stockists), and at the time of writing is available in a range of natural colours ranging from light creams and greys through to dark browns.

This sample contrasts sharply with the crisper patterns achieved with smoother yarns, and could be worked together in a collection of garments, for example a lightweight cotton and silk undersweater and a jacket in alpaca.

Sample 7 (fig 68) – a design suitable for a lightweight cardigan
Set Tension 3/3. Full-needle Jacquard 41 stitches main bed, 40 stitches on the ribber.
Section 1:
Cigno Black mohair (Yeoman Yarns) (A)
Dawn Superkid mohair/nylon Shade 5 (Celandine) (B)
Cigno Cream mohair (Yeoman yarns) (C)
Sienna silk/cotton/acrylic Shade 4 (Celandine) (D)

Fig 68. *Sample 7, Pattern M. Lightweight version of Fig 67. Double-bed Jacquard.*

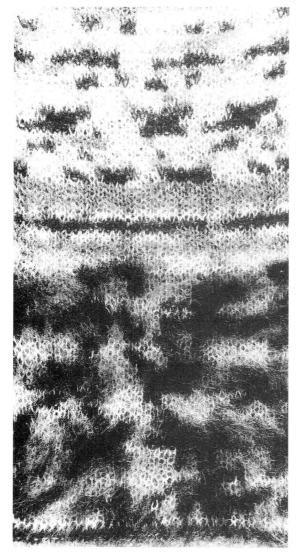

Use the Cream and Ochre mohair to make up a background of random stripes, while knitting the pattern in Black.

Section 2
Dawn superkid mohair/nylon Shade 4 (Celandine) (A)
Dawn superkid mohair/nylon Shade 5 (Celandine) (B)
Cigno Cream mohair (C)
Sienna silk/cotton/acrylic Shade 4 (Celandine) (D)

Using other yarns suitable for Jacquard

With this set of samples, I take a general look at yarns suited to double-bed Jacquard. I have also pursued the idea of altering the number of needles in WP on the main bed to produce ridged fabrics where both sections of knit and purl stitches are visible on the right side.

It is also possible to vary the weight of a particular piece of knitting taking selected needles out of WP into NWP on the rib-bed, for example every alternate or every third needle. This is particularly applicable to models of machine which knit every needle on every row on the ribber. It not only produces a lighter weight fabric, but can be an economical method of producing Jacquard. Commercially produced knitwear sometimes employs this method, leaving small areas of floating yarn next to normally knitted stitches.

It is possible to knit very fine, but relatively stable knitting using fine industrial weight yarns on the double-bed Jacquard machine. A wider range of yarns is becoming available for the home knitter on some of the standard shade cards.

Sample 8 (fig 70) – using finer yarns
This sample uses the following shades:

Black Opium (Yeoman Yarns) (A)
Brown Silki (Bramwell) (B)
Brown/Orange Silki (Bramwell) (C)
Cream Silki (Bramwell) (D)

Pattern N is used throughout, knitted at Tension 2/2 over 71 stitches (*i.e.* 36 needles to the left of centre of the main needle-bed centre, 35 needles to the right).

All samples are cast on using a full-needle rib, with the pitch lever set to half-pitch.

Several rows of stripes using all four colours are knitted. The punchcard or electronic sheet is set to

Fig 69. *Pattern graph N (single bed pattern card).*

the starting position, with the carriage on the correct side of the needle-bed. The pattern sequence is as follows:

Row Counter	Colour
000–002	D
002–004	C
004–006	D
006–008	B
008–010	D
010–012	A
012–014	D
014–016	B
016–018	D
018–020	C

Repeat from 000–020 three times in all, making a total of 60 rows, then continue as follows:

Rows	Colour
060–062	A
062–064	D
064–066	B
066–068	D
068–070	C
070–072	D
072–074	A
074–076	D
076–078	A
078–080	D
080–082	B
082–084	D
084–086	A
086–088	D
088–090	C

Rows 090–110 are as rows 000–020.
Knit several rows of full-needle rib, then cast off.

Sample 9 (fig 71) – a variation
The second sample in this group uses a different range of yarns. They are as follows:

White Elsa (Yeoman Yarns) (A)
Silver Elsa (Yeoman Yarns) (B)
Cream Silki (Bramwell) (C)
Brown/Orange Silki (Bramwell) (D)

This sample follows exactly the same row sequence as the first sample. The tension and number of stitches are also the same.

Sample 10 (fig 72) – a more elaborate variation
This sample is a variation both in the yarns used and the sequence of rows. The four yarns are:

Black Opium (Yeoman) (A)
Charcoal Cigno (Yeoman) (B)
Dark Brown Silki (Bramwell) (C)
Cream Cigno (Yeoman) (D)

Knit to row 060 from the original chart, then follow these instructions to row 080:

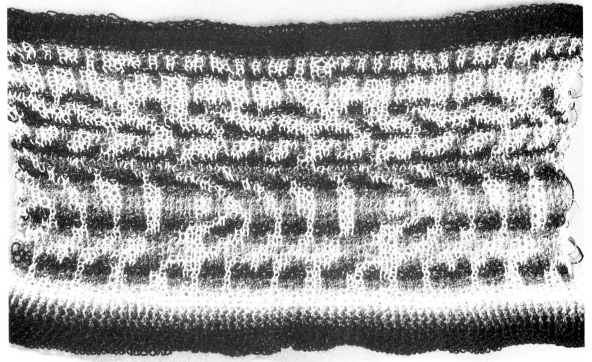

Top left **Fig 70.** *Sample 8, Pattern N. Double-bed Jacquard.*

Bottom left **Fig 71.** *Sample 9, Pattern N. Double-bed Jacquard.*

Row Counter	Colour
060–062	D
062–064	D
064–066	B
066–068	D
068–070	C
070–072	D
072–074	A
074–076	C
076–078	B
078–080	D

Rows 080–110 are as in all the previous samples. This completes one full repeat of the patterns. Continue knitting as follows:

Row Counter	Colour
110–112	C
112–114	D
114–116	B
116–118	D
118–120	A
120–122	D
122–124	B
124–126	D
126–128	C
128–130	D

Knit several rows of full-needle rib in Colour D, then cast off.

Samples – Group 3
This group of samples continues using the same pattern, but the samples allow you to look at varying qualities and weights of yarn, as well as the effect of

Fig 72. *Sample 10, Pattern N. Double-bed Jacquard.*

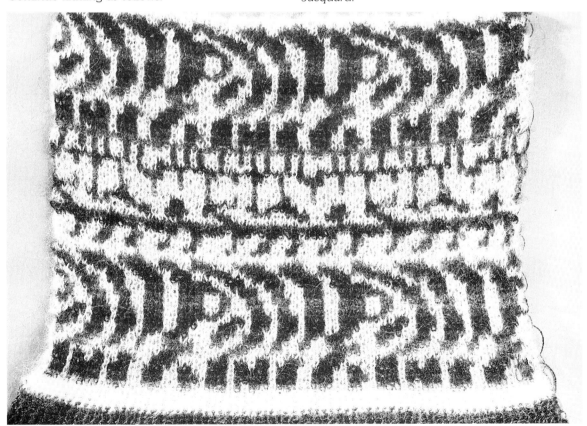

altering the number of needles in WP on the main bed.

Sample 11 (fig 73) – using two colours only
Both yarns are 100% acrylic from the Lovat collection by F.W. Bramwell (see list of stockists):

Dark Grey (A)
Beige (B)

The sample is knitted at Tension 6/6 over 71 stitches. The main bed is as follows:

Fig 73. *Sample 11, Pattern N. Double-bed Jacquard.*

KH X X X X O X X X X O X X X O etc.
KR X X X X X X X X X X X X X etc.
(X = WP; O = NWP; KH = main bed; KR = ribber; note half-pitch)

One complete repeat of the pattern is knitted. The centre 24 needles are left as for the first part of the sample, but needles to the left and right of this section are all put back into WP. A second repeat of the pattern is then knitted, followed by several rows of full-needle rib if required. Finally cast off.

Sample 12 (fig 74)
The second sample of this group uses two colours of silk by Gaddum (see stockists list), and a white pure wool of similar weight.

Set Tension 6/6. Use white wool. Knit 20 rows of circular knitting.
Use Tension 6/6, white wool. Knit 4 rows full-needle rib.
Transfer the needles as follows, working from left to right across the needle-bed.

KH   X X X O O O   (3 needles in WP)
KR   X X X X X
(note half pitch)

Fig 74. *Sample 12, Pattern N. Double-bed Jacquard with alternate needle settings on the main bed.*

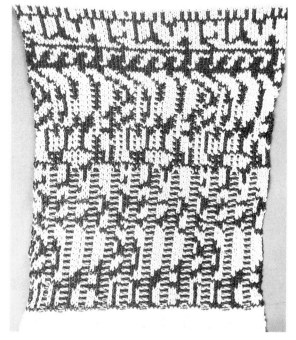

i.e. 3 needles in WP, and 3 needles in NWP. The empty needles are achieved by transferring stitches down to the ribber bed using a double-eyed transfer tool.

Knit 8 rows in White at Tension 6/6 in this arrangement.

Insert pattern card or set the electronic sheet to the starting line.

Knit one complete pattern of 110 rows in this needle arrangement.

Change the needle setting to:

KH   X X X O X O   etc.   (2 needles in WP)
KR   X X X X X X etc.
(note half-pitch)

Set the row counter to 000.
Push the remaining needles on the main bed into WP

and knit a full Jacquard for the remainder of the pattern. On row 072 swap foreground and background until Rows 088–110. Colours as before. Knit several rows in full-needle rib in White wool and cast off.

Sample 13 (fig 75)
The third sample looks at another way of varying the needle arrangement, this time to make broader bands of knit-facing pattern contrasting with purl-facing birdseye texture.

Four colours are used:

Silk – Pale pink (Gaddums) (A)
Silk – Dark blue (Gaddums) (B)
50% Mink/50% Lambswool – Quality Karen in No 7 (Celandine) (C)
50% Mink/50% Lambswool – Quality Karen in No 6 (Celandine) (D)

Cast on 101 stitches in A and knit 4 rows.
Change to white wool, knit another 4 rows.

Fig 75. *Fine lightweight double-bed Jacquard, using an alternate needle setting on the main bed, in silk yarns and a 50% lambswool, 50% mink mix.*

Then arrange the needles in the following setting:

```
KH  X X X X X O O O O O  etc.
KR    X X X X X X X X X X etc.
```
(note half pitch)

Row Counter	Colour
000–002	A
002–004	B
004–006	A
006–008	C
008–010	A
010–012	D

This sequence is repeated until Row 050, ending on A. Continue as follows:

Row Counter	Colour
050–052	A
052–054	B
054–056	B
056–058	A
058–060	B
060–062	A
062–064	C
064–066	A
066–068	D

Repeat Rows 056–068 until Row 085 is reached, and then:

Row Counter	Colour
086–088	B
088–090	B
090–092	D
092–094	B

Repeat rows 090–094 until Row 110 is reached. This ends one repeat of the pattern.

For the next section, reset the row counter to 000. Follow 000–036 from the first section of this sample and then:

Row Counter	Colour
036–038	B
038–040	B
040–042	C
042–044	B

Repeat Rows 040–044 four times in all (Row 056) ending on B, and finally:

Row Counter	Colour
056–058	D
058–060	B

Repeat Rows 056–060 six times in all, then Cast off.

Sample 14 (fig 76)
Knit 30 rows of 2-up, 2-down rib at Tension 3/3 over 71 stitches, using White wool.

```
KH  X X O X X O X X
KR    O X X O X X O
```
(X = WP, O = NWP, note half pitch)

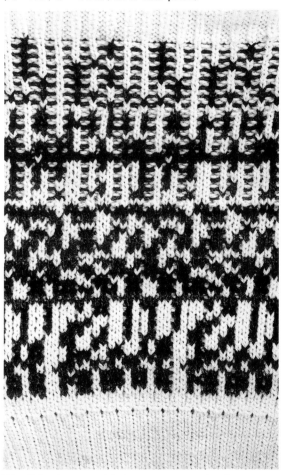

Fig 76. *Sample 14, Pattern N. Double-bed Jacquard with alternate needle settings on the main bed.*

Fig 77. *Sample 15, Pattern N. Double-bed Jacquard with alternate needle settings on the main bed.*

Knit 3 Rows White wool, Tension 3/3. Carriage on Left.
Set up for Jacquard knitting using Pattern No Colours as follows:

Black cotton crepe (Texere Yarns) (A)
Blue mix, 4-ply Cotton/Botany (Brockwell Yarns) (B)
Blue Silk (Gaddum) (C)
White pure wool (D)

Set Tension 5/5.
Rows 000–002, D, and *every alternate pair of rows*. Colours A, B and C are chosen at random on the remaining alternate pairs of rows, until row 40. This ends with Colour C. 040–042 are also in C.
Continue as before with D on every alternate pair of rows, until Row 080.
Rearrange main bed needles thus:

KH X X O X O O X X O X O O etc.
KR   X X X X X X X X X X X X etc.
(note half-pitch)

Continue knitting in the same manner starting with D until Row 100, which ends on A.
Rows 100–102 are also A.
Continue as before until Row 120, which ends on D.
Rearrange the main bed needles thus:

KH X O O X O O X O O X O O etc.
KR   X X X X X X X X X X X etc.
(note half-pitch)

Commence knitting with D in the same type of sequence until Row 150. Knit several rows in White.
Transfer to main bed.
Cast off.

Sample 15 (fig 77)
30 Rows 2-up 1-down Rib.
Push into WP all ribber needles, and move the ribber one full pitch to the left.

Knit 2 rows in White.
Set up yarns thus:

Hibiscus (Atkinson) (A)
Multi-coloured fleck Lurex. (B)

Knit in alternate rows. Swap background and foreground colours at regular intervals.

Sample 16 (fig 78)
The final sample is a fantasy Jacquard using white Chenille, two types of Butterfly yarn from Yeoman Yarns, and a black and white Slub Cotton from Brockwell. The colours were changed totally at random to produce a blurred pattern and a range of samples all from one card using different yarns and needle settings. There are many more variations for you to try.

If you own an electronic machine, variation in scale and positioning of the pattern can add another dimension to your sampling. Four samples using a pure wool from Many-A-Mickle illustrate this point, producing a very wearable winter-weight knit (see figs 59, 60, 61).

Jacquard as a technique does require a little patience to understand, but once you have overcome this barrier it is possible to produce many beautiful fabrics varying in weight, surface texture and application.

Fig 78. *Sample 16, Pattern N. Double-bed Jacquard with alternate needle settings on the main bed.*

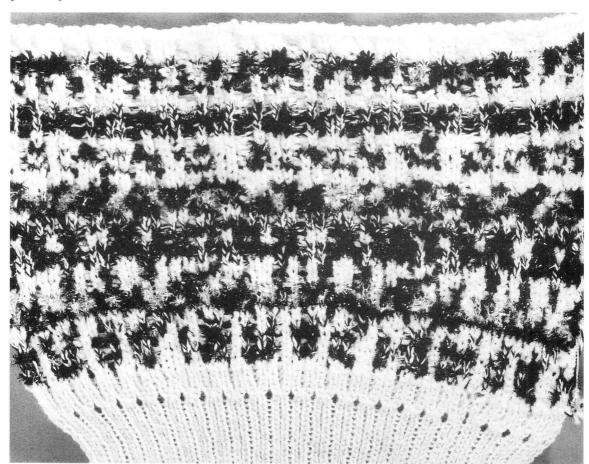

CHAPTER 3
Designing for two-colour knitting

As a knitter you will most probably have worked through the sets of patterns made available with your model of machine. Or you will have tried some of the examples included earlier in the book, but you may still feel very much a newcomer to the world of designing.

There are many ways of approaching the production of your own pattern, each way having its own merits; and the way that you choose will depend upon your particular capablities. If you have never designed for pattern before, start with a simple idea and build on it gradually, as you most probably did when you were first learning the basic machine techniques. Don't worry unduly if you are not a practised draughtsman. I will suggest shortcuts and more mechanical ways of working, such as the use of tracings, photocopies, and various grid-based systems.

Try out new ideas, and enjoy the challenge of producing something identifiably your own. At the same time keep a close eye on how other knitters and/or designers approach working with pattern and colour, as well as the traditional applications mentioned in Chapter 1.

Look at modern hand-knit designers – Kaffe Fassett has probably become the most well known since his excellent television series was broadcast. He makes an art out of knitting, using a richly graduated pallette and complex patterns.

Look also at the work of the Natural Dye Company, who specialize in hand-knitted garments using natural dye colours and traditional-style patterns using silks, wools and cottons.

Yoshimi Kihara knits soft blends of pattern and colour to produce subtle, almost abstract imagery – sometimes using her own hand-dyed yarns. Sasha Kagan (based in Wales) concentrates on decorative surfaces, quite often combining geometric and figurative motifs. Susan Duckworth uses popular folk-art and rural imagery in a rich range of colours and textures utilizing geometric and floral styles.

Martin Kidman, who has designed for Joseph Tricot, produces richly patterned handknits, and

Fig 79. *Example of a two-colour pattern, single-bed method, knitted in contrasting shades of silk.*

sometimes incorporates Swiss darning to embellish the pattern. Early examples of his work were inspired by Persian carpets – a design source which many knitters, myself included, have used. Some of Carrie White's work includes features and motifs reminis-

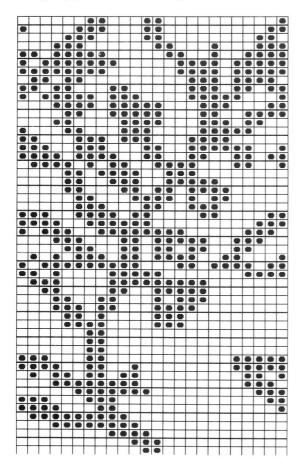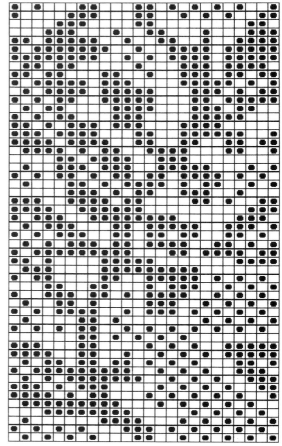

Fig 80. *Pattern graph for Fig 79, before an addition of a speckled background.*

Fig 81. *Pattern graph for Fig 79, after the background has been added.*

cent of Middle-eastern carpet designs. She knits in wools, silks and chenilles, mainly by machine, and incorporates large panels of pattern.

In complete contrast Boyd and Boyd use stark, geometric patterns in strongly contrasting colours. Among the new generation of British designers, Rosemary Moore has produced bold designs in black and white, based on African masks, for computer-controlled machine knits in MAXXAM fabric.

There are also knitted carpets from the seventeenth and eighteenth centuries. One example (from Alsace) is in the Victoria and Albert Museum in London and several European museums also have examples. You can compare them with modern work by designers such as Rene Dymtrenko, who makes machine knitted bedspreads worked in strips of pattern. Examples of her work can be seen in the Crafts Council's knit slides-pack.

Keep a watchful eye on such periodicals as *Vogue Knitting* or *Crafts* magazine, as they quite often feature leading designers. Check out the fashion papers, too, and try to visit trade shows and craft fairs if the general public are allowed access.

Many designers produce knit-kits and patterns for particular magazines, and local Art and Craft galleries occasionally show exhibitions of designer knitwear. These are always worth a visit, as are demonstrations by working craftspeople.

Before tackling the problem of just how you are going to make your own design, take a close look at the types of patterns that will suit, first, the technique you are intending to use, and second the limitations imposed by your machine on the size of pattern repeat.

I have already mentioned the problem of floating yarns stranding across the back of single-bed patterned knitting. So, a small-scale all-over repeat pattern, or a small motif, would be a good starting point for a design. You can gradually work towards designing larger scale patterns. These have to be carefully organized so that the main images do not lose their clarity. The float problem means you have to break up the images, maybe by arranging a speckled background using colours A and B in rapid succession, rather than one large area of a single colour.

This type of designing needs practice. You will probably find that your first attempts are not quite what you had hoped for. A common problem is that the design becomes too cluttered and broken up, with the main features lost against an overcomplicated background. Or the balance between light and dark or foreground and background is too similar.

I have included a 'before and after' graph here. The first one (fig 80) shows the image of a stem with leaves and small flowers against a plain background. The second example shows one solution to the problem (fig 81).

It is worth noting that if the outcome of your designing is large, bold images spaced across a plain background, then you should look toward the intarsia technique as a way of working the design in knit, if you do not want to modify the pattern to any great extent.

Double-bed Jacquard is the other answer. The outcome will depend very much on the type of knitted fabric you require, and its suitability for the purpose.

Clearly if you are working to produce only double-bed designs then some of the previous limitations do not arise, as the float problem is eliminated whichever double-bed system you employ.

Aesthetic concerns remain important. Although the shapes in the design can in theory be as large as the machine will allow, questions of proportion and balance, and distribution of pattern over the knitted area, are still of great relevance.

Suggested Themes for Design Ideas

First choose a theme from which to work. This should be capable of providing ideas for both pattern shapes and colour. This will depend a lot upon whether you want to start completely from scratch, or use 'ready-made' motifs to which you can add your own personal touch.

If you decide to go for the latter, you might consider

Fig 82. *Example of a 2-colour pattern (single-bed method) knitted in contrasting textures, based on leaves and electronic circuit boards.*

Paisley patterns, Art Nouveau, floral designs, medieval or other early decorative textiles, Coptic weaves, various folk-art motifs, Islamic decoration, Ikat weaving, Art Deco designs, or mosaic patterns. The local library can be a good source of information, especially if it has a section on historical textiles and the decorative arts.

If you want to start from scratch from your own drawings or photographs, suggested themes could include ready-made images that already have a pattern-like quality. In the past I have used photos taken around docks and building sites. The cranes and hoists, scaffolding and girders and so forth found

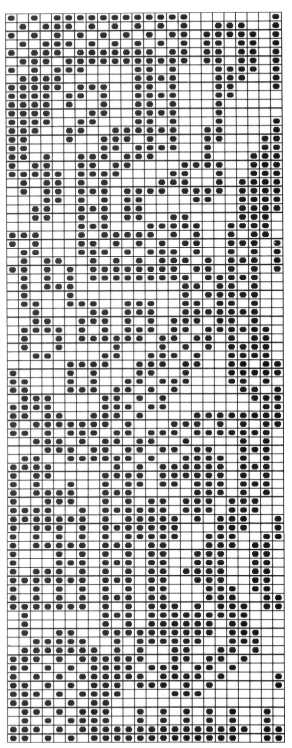

Fig 83. *Example of a 2-colour pattern (single-bed method) showing a normal and elongated version in fine, smooth wools (dark blue and white) using leaf patterns as inspiration.*

Fig 84. *Pattern graph for Fig 82. 24-stitch repeat.*

in these places make very interesting shapes, which can then be developed as repeat or single-unit designs. Other good sources are railway junctions (look at the lines and signals), telegraph wires and pylons, buildings generally, tiles, brickwork, wrought iron, groups of buildings, groups of windows in a building (see fig 86).

Of course, your tastes may not be so starkly urban, and you may prefer to take your camera or

Fig 85. *Pattern graph for Fig 83. 24-stitch repeat.*

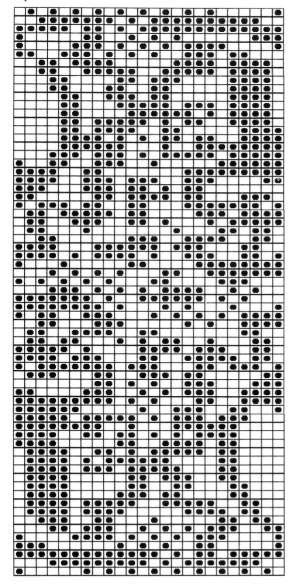

sketchbook to the quayside, where you will find fishing nets, lobster pots and related tackle, fish, fish-boxes, interesting stonework, boats and their rigging, and the water itself.

You might also like to look at aerial photographs, maps, circuit diagrams, lettering on posters and signs, old faded photographs, seaside postcards, stamp collections, animal markings, or patterns in crystals and rocks such as marble.

Perhaps you might decide that the pattern will come from one source, and the colour from another, or to use a theme that you have already started to develop for another technique. Treated sympathetically, the same source material can be used with any number of suitable methods, enabling the knitter to produce a range of samples related through colour content, pattern, or both.

This approach has many advantages, especially if you are working commercially on a collection, or a complete outfit in which a common linking factor, for example colour or pattern, is required. I particularly like to work out patterns for small-scale repetitive designs suited to both Jacquard and single-bed techniques, which can also be carried over into other areas such as intarsia work on a chunky-gauge machine.

A jacket could be designed making use of the intarsia pattern, perhaps with ribbed insets; a matching skirt or sweater could be knitted in Jacquard.

Finding a Method of Working for Simple Pattern Design

Having organized a suitable theme to work from, and surrounded yourself with useful reference material, it is a good idea to try out several approaches to designing your own patterns. You will need to find a method of working that you feel comfortable with, and that suits your own style and capabilities.

No two designers work in exactly the same manner even though there is a common aim – in this case to find a way of visualizing ideas for pattern, and ultimately to produce a punchcard or mylar sheet for the machine.

If you are fortunate enough to be working with a computer-aided system then much of the work can be done on the system's display screen, by way of some input device (such as a 'mouse' or via the computer keyboard – see fig 87), but the same basic principles apply. In whatever way you should decide to work, the first objective is to design a single pattern unit

Fig 86. *Ideas from the author's sketchbook, showing decorative architectural features.*

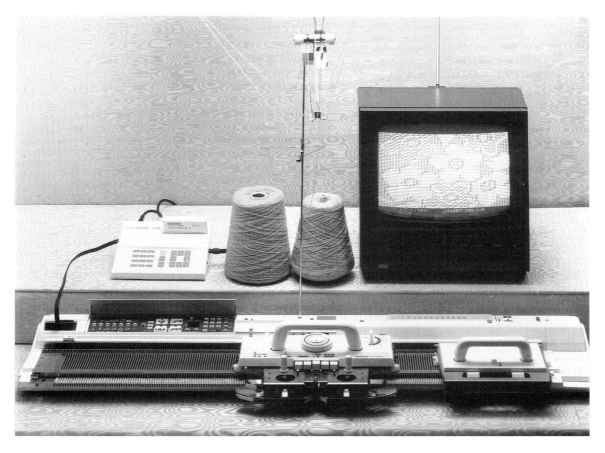

Fig 87. *Brother 9501 Electronic machine with PPD11O.*

which you can then play around with to generate a series of simple repeated motifs.

Before starting any design work, check that you are familiar with the overall size of the pattern repeat system for your machine. Here are some examples, starting with the manual-selection and punchcard machines.

12 stitches manual selection on some Toyotas. Also applicable to the Chunky Knitmaster 155.

24 stitches Standard punchcard size for Brother, Knitmaster, and some Toyota machines. The KH 260 Brother Chunky also uses standard 24 stitch repeat.

40 stitches The Deco system of the Pfaff or Passap utilises this system.

Looking now at the electronic machines:

60 stitches The Brother 910 and 950 work to this 150 row system, as does the standard Knitmaster Electronic.

200 stitches The Design Master Electronic from Knitmaster, in conjunction with the PE1 Design Controller Memory Box allows the use of some or all of the 200 needles.

The Brother 950I is capable of knitting a single pattern repeat ranging from 1–200 stitches wide. This can use either a Mylar sheet or be linked to the new PPD110 (Pattern Programming Device) – an accessory which, rather like a home computer, can be plugged into the aerial socket of your TV set, allowing you to build up designs directly on to the screen.

The Pfaff Electronic 6000 patterns can also use the full machine if required, as each needle is controlled independently. There are therefore no maximum or minimum stitch repeats (see fig 88).

I suggest as a starting point, that a unit of pattern is

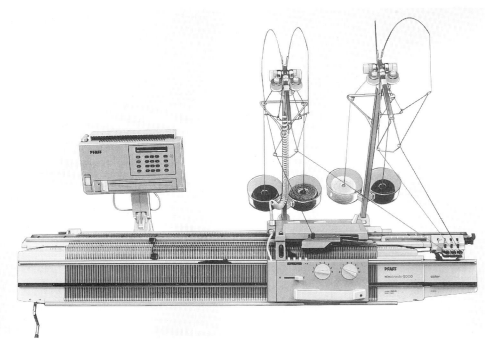

Fig 88.
Pfaff Electronic 6000.

devised that is equally divisible into the total number of units in your particular repeat system. So, the overall pattern repeats can be broken down into the following smaller units:

8 stitches: 1, 2, 4 or 8 stitch units.
12 stitches: 1, 2, 3, 4, 6 or 12 stitch units.
24 stitches: as for 12, but also 8 and 24 units.
40 stitches: as for 8, and also 5, 10, 20, and 40.

As far as the Electronic machines are concerned, the repeat unit can be any number between either 1 and 60 or 1 and 200 depending upon the machine. However, be careful when working out extra-large patterns for repeat designs. Say, for example, you designed a pattern that was 55 stitches total width. When put into repeat, and in order not to lose some of the pattern, the knitter should cast on either 55, 110 or 165 stitches. This can be a limitation unless the garment as a whole is designed with this difficulty borne in mind.

A repeat of, say, 6 stitches gives a lot more potential for variation, since the total number of stitches to be cast on can be any multiple of six (12, 18, 24 etc).

Returning to the point about size of pattern unit, a good method of working is to outline a series of boxes on graph-paper, the units of which are evenly divisible into the overall number of the full repeat.

The example of a 24 stitch repeat gives a potential baseline of 2, 3, 4, 6, 8, 12 or 24 stitches. A pattern

shape can then be designed to fit neatly into this outline. Working in this way ensures that the pattern shape goes readily into repeat without any more redrawing. Once a successful shape has been devised, it can be copied out x number of times to fit the punchcard, or once only if for the Electronic machine. For an illustration of the process, see fig 89.

The 4 stitch by 12 row repeat is drawn out six times in order to fill the punchcard. As you have probably realized, the punchcard must be filled with a design across the full width of the repeat.

Fig 89. *4 stitch × 12 row pattern unit in a simple block repeat format.*

78

Designing a suitable shape for repeat patterns

You will need a selection of soft pencils (2B or 3B), a rubber and some proportional graph-paper. I have included an example at the end of the book which you can photocopy. I always try to use this graph-paper rather than the usual squared type. If you use the latter, the final knitted image will have a squat, wide appearance because in most circumstances a knit stitch is not square (especially in plain-knit structures). The vertical size is less than the horizontal size in a ratio of about 4:5.

Outline a series of boxes in an appropriate size for your repeat system. Then using the visual references you have collected as a starting point, draw freehand within the box or trace off the outlines of self-contained shapes. Try to vary the size, form and character of each shape (see fig 90).

Fig 90. *Ideas for pattern shapes.*

Try to give each type of shape you are drawing different characteristics. For example tall, small, long, rounded, leaning, jagged and spiky, and so on. Much of this will depend upon your source information. If you are having difficulty in drawing freehand the type of shapes you like, use the Dawson's Grid© (see Chapter 4) and work directly from the photos, drawings or whatever you are using.

If you are designing for single-bed knitting, it is important to limit the width of the pattern-shapes to around eight units across at any one point. This reduces the problem of overlong floats on the reverse side of the knitting. Naturally the height of the motif is not limited in the same way. If the design is for double-bed Jacquard, then these limitations can be ignored. I would suggest here that you try to design a group of shapes that vary considerably in size. This will eventually give you scope to complete quite complex patterns using several contrasting shapes together in one pattern.

Once you have a series of outlines on the graph-

paper, a stepped image needs to be produced working stitch by stitch and row by row. Look at fig 91(a) and then at fig 91(b). These explain the next part of the process.

Remember that the graph is a diagram on which 1 unit equals 1 stitch or row. Also, the actual *size* of the graph bears no relation to the size of the final knitted piece. The same graph can be used for hand-knitting ultra-thick yarn on very large needles, or machine-knitting fine yarns at a very tight tension.

So far you have compiled a series of outlined shapes. Rework some of them as solid blocks, filling in all the squares enclosed by the outline. Another variation is to fill out *every* alternate square on *every* row to make a chequerboard a speckled birdseye pattern within the main shape. Again make the

outline 2 or 3 units deep all around the edge or vary the thickness of the outline (fig 92).

At this stage, you will have different versions of the same basic shape. This is one way to vary the overall appearance of a design; emphasizing some shapes and letting others go to the background.

Fig 91a. *Pattern shape as a line drawing.*

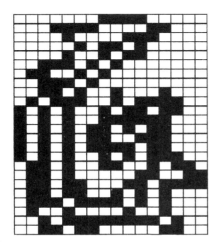

Fig 91b. *Pattern converted to a blocked-in graph.*

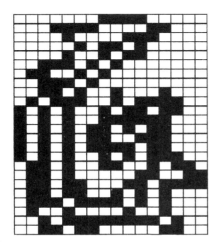

Fig 93. *Simple block repeat format, using one pattern unit as the building-block. Unit of repeat: 8 stitches × 18 rows.*

Now choose one particular favourite shape and repeat it as a block across the full repeat (fig 93). A very simple variation is to then make Repeat B a solid shape, and A and C an outlined shape (fig 94). Alternatively the background of A and C could be a solid colour similar to the pattern in Band D (see fig 95). Try a number of different arrangements.

Varying the design format

The only experience you have had so far of making a composite pattern is by making a block repeat where A, B, C is the unit of repeat of, say, 8 stitches wide by 18 rows deep (fig 93).

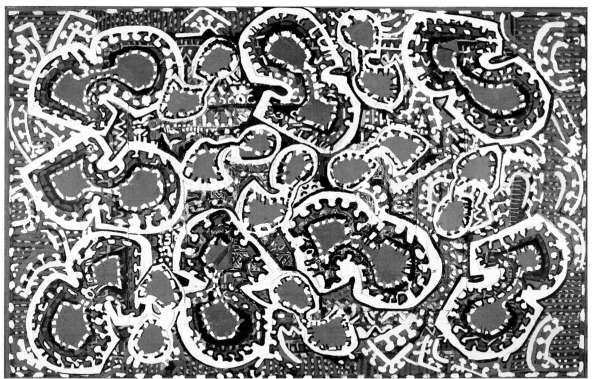
Design idea for an Intarsia knit

Colour and tension swatches for an Intarsia knit. Several fine ends
of yarn have been plyed together to achieve various blends of colour

Colourboard based on the 'garden theme' showing various groupings
of colours in sixteen-unit chequerboard samples, edged with windings
of yarn in differing proportions and colour

Intarsia jacket knitted on the chunky gauge machine with fine gauge
double-bed Jacquard sleeves; worn over a lightweight ribbed dress

Jacket knitted in double-bed Jacquard and knitweave using a mixture of cottons, fine mohair type yarns, industrial weight lurex and chenille. The skirt is ribbed using a combination of fine wools and lurex

Co-ordinating sweater and skirt knitted in double-bed Jacquard and a broad, two-colour plated rib; worked in wools, cottons, Atkinsons Geneve and chenille type yarn

left Slitted jacket (vertical slit method using partial knit) worked in single bed patterned knit technique and incorporating 'knitted-in' bobbles. The sleeves are knitted in an all-over tuck stitch pattern

Suit knitted in double-bed Jacquard and incoporating panels
of two-colour ribbing worked in fine wools, cottons and chenille
type yarn

right Strip sweater in reds and maroons knitted in contrasting textures
of yarn; a detachable pleated collar and a pleated, quilted evening
wrap shown alongside a section of a slitted cardigan worked in shades
of blues, greens and purples

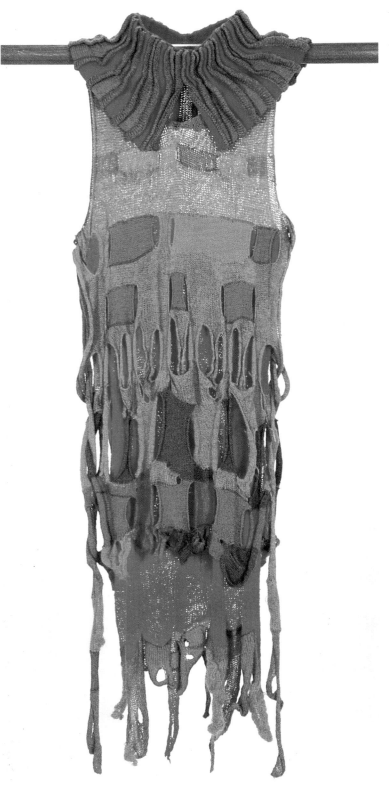

left Dress knitted in ochre silk, fine red wool and silk mix, blue cotton and fine wool using the vertical slitted surface technique

right Bodice of dress using the partial knit technique for the patterned centre front panel and shaped frill, knitted in cottons, slubs, rayons, wools and chenille type yarn

Section of jacket

left Jacket showing horizontal, slitted surfaces (drawn thread method), single-bed two colour patterned knitting, plain knit and multi-coloured plated ribbing

Double-bed Jacquard evening wrap knitted in fine wools and
industrial weight lurex worn over a machine knitted and embroidered
jacket and co-ordinating ribbed dress

right Double-bed Jacquard jacket with knitweave yoke and co-
ordinating skirt knitted in wools, fine lurex, mohair and chenille
type yarns and Atkinsons Geneve

Strip coat. Plain knit wool base with knitted in patterned strips,
using a mixture of wools, cottons, chenilles, slub and boucle yarns

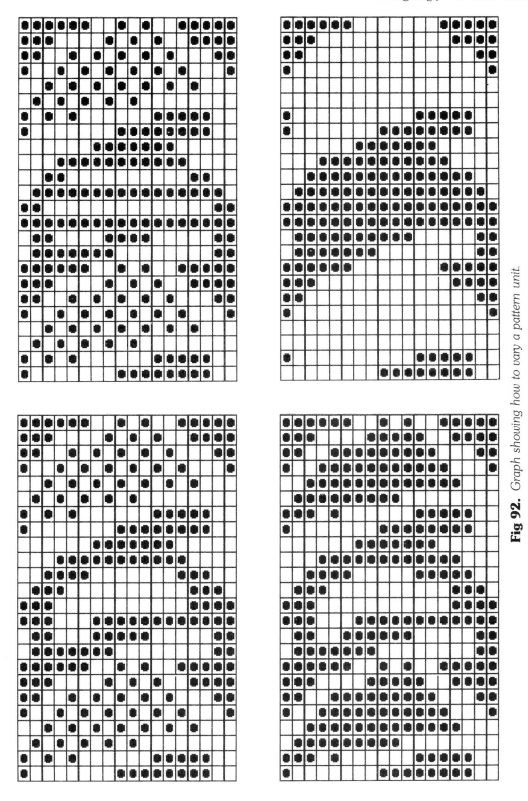

Fig 92. *Graph showing how to vary a pattern unit.*

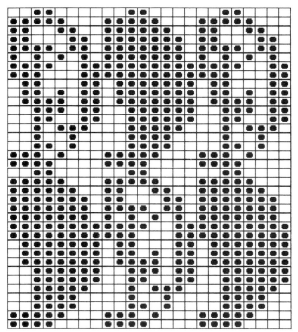

Fig 94. *Block repeat format – solid and outlined patterns for use as a 16 stitch overall repeat (Electronics).*

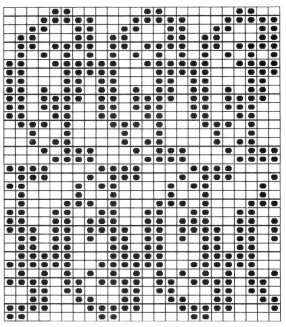

Fig 96. *Brick repeat structure using one pattern unit. The second row of images is made into a reflection suitable for a 24 stitch repeat.*

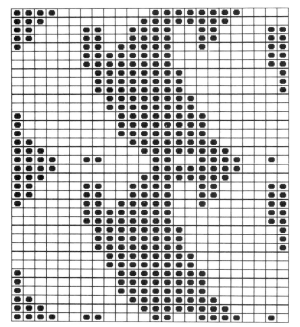

Fig 95. *Block repeat format – negative and positive silhouettes for use as a 16 stitch overall repeat (Electronics).*

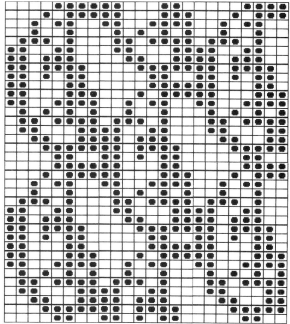

Fig 97. *Half-drop repeat structure using one pattern unit for use as a 16 stitch overall repeat (Electronics).*

The same unit can be offset so that the second vertical repeat of the pattern moves the starting point 4 stitches to the right. It could have been moved one, two or three places to the right. Try some other variations (see fig 96). The 18 rows could then be repeated as many times as required.

If you have been designing for the 40-stitch repeat for the Deco unit on the Pfaff then you will only need to draw out, for example, 12 rows by 40 stitches. The design can be centred anywhere over the 40-stitch repeat.

Once you have your design, you can knit Repeat A, then move the centre of the design 4 stitches to the left and knit Repeat B. A one-stitch movement left or right is possible at any time. The Electronic machines allow for the same type of movement by programming in a new first-needle position.

Obviously with the mechanically operated punchcard machines the new position of the pattern has to be drawn on to and punched out of the card. Other simple variations involve offsetting alternate columns of pattern.

In fig 97, for example, columns 2, 4 and 6 have their baseline of the first full block of pattern at Row 10. The pattern unit can also be flipped over (fig 98), turned upside down or made as a reflection (fig 99).

Fig 99. *Block repeat structure using one pattern unit, but with the second row of images made into a reflected image suitable for a 24 stitch repeat.*

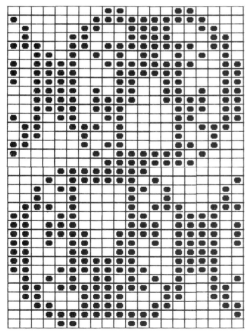

Fig 98. *Brick repeat structure, using one pattern unit. Alternative units facing left, other alternative units facing right.*

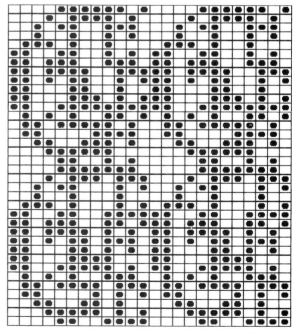

Fig 100. *Introducing a new pattern unit of 4 stitches × 18 rows to combine with the original single unit of 8 stitches × 18 rows. Use as a 24 stitch repeat.*

Fig 101. *Development of Fig 100.*

Right **Fig 102.** *Diagram giving method of checking that the left and right, and top and bottom, edges of a pattern line up correctly when put into full repeat.*

Experiment with some of your favourite shapes to produce several ideas for small repeat patterns. A simple way of extending the small, formal repeat type patterns is to introduce another shape to replace some of the original units. In fig 100, every other unit is the original pattern shape but each unit between is the new shape. The next example extends the idea (fig 101).

Once you are totally satisfied with a design, rub out all the grid lines surrounding the pattern or redraw it, then transfer the image to punchcard or Electronic paper. If you are working directly with the computer, store the pattern in the computer-memory for later use.

An important consideration at this stage is to check that both left and right sides of the pattern match perfectly, as do the top and bottom edges. Make sure that there are no unsightly and disjointed linking areas.

To check these points, either trace the complete design or photocopy it. You will need to do this four times (fig 102).

This produces a rough visual of how the pattern will appear in repeat. Don't forget that the graph is only a diagram, and does not represent the actual size of the finished knitted piece.

If you happen to know roughly how many rows and stitches make up 1cm of knitting, it is possible to calculate approximately the size of, say, 24 stitches. Using a photocopier that reduces or enlarges, it may be possible to obtain a rough that is nearly correct in size and would relate more closely to how the finished piece would look.

If at this stage the pattern does not link correctly, draw on the photocopies and redesign the joining edges. Photocopy again until you are completely satisfied with the result. It is much easier to make corrections at this stage than later when the card has been punched out.

Transferring the design from graph-paper

To transfer the design to a punchcard work row by row, marking with a pencil either the negative or positive areas. It is best to mark that which is the least total area to save unnecessary work. It makes no difference which areas are punched out as the yarn can be swapped between the yarn-feeds.

It is easier to follow the graph if two sheets of paper are used to cover the areas of graph on either side of the row being drawn out, to isolate that particular row.

Once you have marked all the cards, punch out the appropriate areas.

Make sure that each hole is centrally located in its square. Misalignment can result in the mechanism ignoring the hole completely and knitting the wrong colour stitch.

Refer to the section of your instruction manual which deals with transferring the image to Mylar sheet, or whichever special paper your electronic machine requires.

If, of course, you are working with a fully computerized system (e.g. DATAKNIT or the PE1 Design Controller for the Knitmaster Design Master) then put the patterns into the machine's memory for future use.

If you are working towards a double-bed pattern, refer to Chapter 2 for the method of converting a design into a suitable punchcard. Check individual Electronic machine manuals – you may find that the same graph will suffice for both methods.

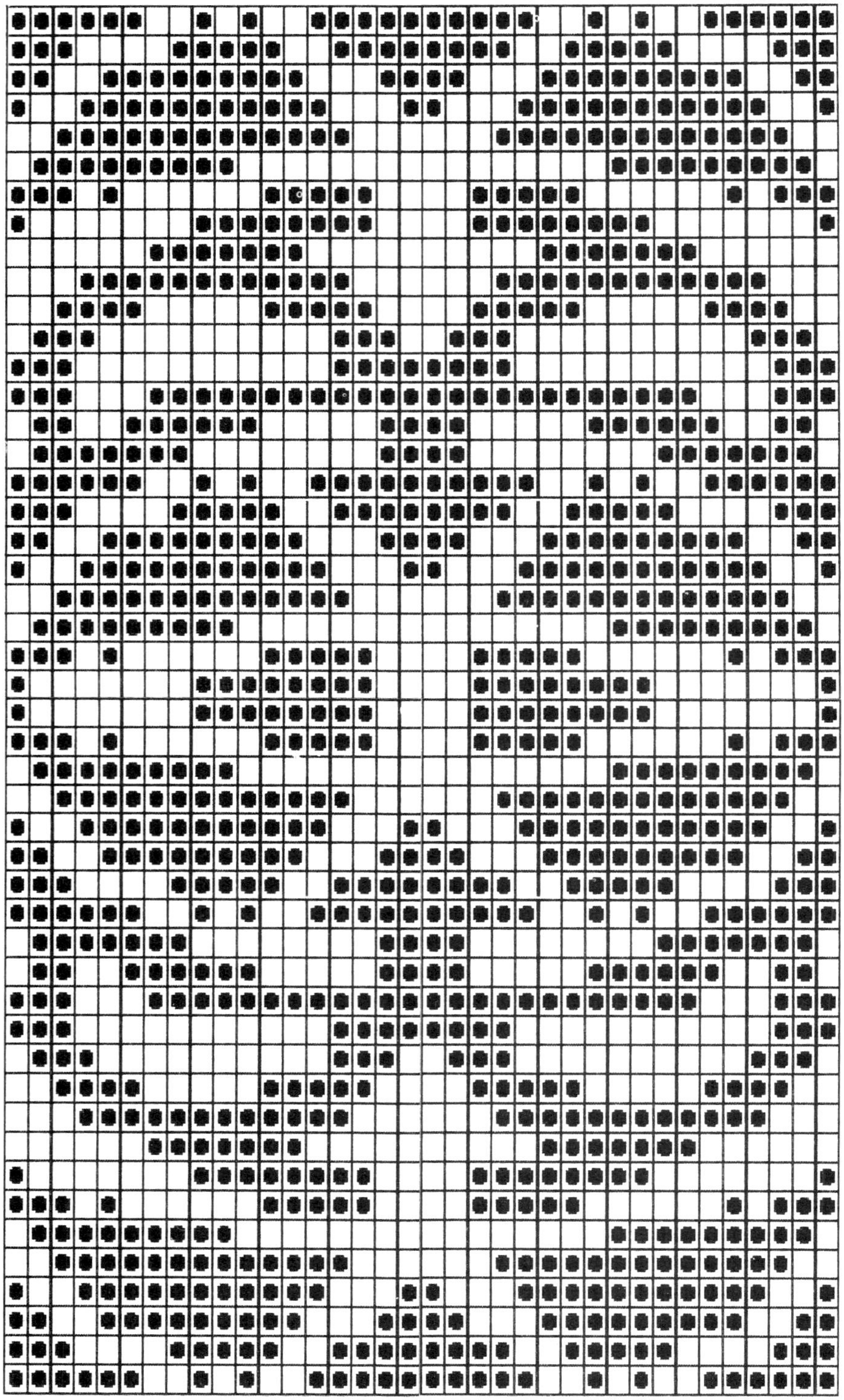

Fig 103. *Large composite pattern.*

Fig 104. *Design motifs for use on the electronic machine.*

You are now ready to start knitting again. Refer back to either the chapter on single-bed pattern card technique, or the double-Jacquard chapter; taking up some of the original ideas on methods discussed when working from my patterns. To help you to extend your ideas even further, a series of more complex patterns follows (see figs 103 and 104). Apply some of these methods to your own designs, gradually adding to your repertoire.

CHAPTER 4
Intarsia knitting

The technique of intarsia knitting is most generally used to interpret multicoloured surface patterns in which the designs either involve more than two colours per row or where the imagery is of such a scale and complexity that it would be impractical to use the two-colour stranded method discussed in Chapter 1.

The word *intarsia* was not originally a knitting term. It meant (as it still does) a decorative process in which small pieces of wood in a variety of colours and grains were inlaid on a wooden surface to produce pictorial

Fig 105. *Close-up section of intarsia jacket (chunky gauge).*

Fig 106. *Section of full-length intarsia coat (chunky gauge).*

effects, and as an art-form reached a peak of development in Renaissance Italy. Intarsia knitting is usually highly decorative; sometimes narrative or pictorial, sometimes pure pattern, and is often produced on a large scale. Originally a hand-knitting technique, the method has been used increasingly by machine-knitters who have made the pleasing discovery that use of a mechanical device does not necessarily restrict the knitter to repetitive figures or the simple geometry of lines and stripes.

With the Intarsia method the creative knitter can produce a wide range of imagery, varying in format, shape, scale and colour. The process allows the machine-knitter a freedom of expression approaching that of the tapestry weaver (see figs 105 and 106).

The Intarsia technique is simple to use and, once mastered, does not get in the way of the creative process. The designer can adopt much the same approach to the work as that of a painter to the canvas. Few restrictions are placed on the number of colours that can be knitted into any given row (ultimately the same as the number of needles in use), so the final design can be as basic or complicated as the individual cares to make it. Subtle colour changes can be worked, or big abstract shapes, detailed motifs, letters, squares and triangles, and so on. It is probably the least mechanical of the design methods available to the machine-knitter, and used imaginatively can produce spectacular results.

The Intarsia Method

The technique produces multicoloured, patterned knitting without floats. Machine-knit Intarsia is constructed by laying in separate ends of colour by hand (each colour is wound on a bobbin). The yarn lies along the required number of needles between the open latch and the hook of each needle.

If a continuously linked piece of fabric is required then it is important that adjacent ends of different coloured yarns are crossed or linked to avoid an unwanted gap. Note that if this procedure is carried out correctly there is no need to uncross the yarns at the end of each row as this will happen naturally on every second row. Do check that the cross-over of yarns falls between, rather than on, the needles.

On the machine, either the purl-face (rough) or the knit-face (smooth) can be used, but it is not possible to have knit and purl stitches in the same row. This is one disadvantage of using machines when compared

Fig 108. *Chunky gauge machine-knit intarsia in silks, cottons and wool. Sample idea for a co-ordinating sweater to complement Fig 107.*

Fig 107. *Example of hand-knit using both purl and knit facing stitches (slip stitch, corrugated ribbing and stranded knit). An idea for a jacket sleeve.*

Fig 109. *Chunky gauge intarsia (top left) co-ordinating with hand-knit samples. Bottom left shows a hand-knit intarsia with knit and purl stitches facing.*

with the hand-knitted equivalent. Any textural variety in machine-knitted Intarsia work must be achieved either through the interplay and variation of textured yarns or by using the garter bar or the waste yarn method, to turn the work.

Alternatively, a section of hand knit of a similar gauge could be incorporated into a machine-knit garment. The illustrations show examples of this (figs 107, 108 and 109).

Choosing the appropriate method

It is of course possible to produce two-colour-per-row designs on a large scale, especially since the development of the electronic machine, through the use of the double-bed Jacquard technique. This turns out fabric with quite a different feel from that produced by single-bed plain knit, which is more flexible and stretchy. Features such as weight, elasticity, drape and the ability to shape easily on the machine should all be taken into account when deciding which method is appropriate.

The largest piece of knitting which the machine is capable of producing (in terms of width) is obviously dictated by the total number of needles available on the individual machine, and the tension set by the knitter. If larger pieces are required, for example bedspreads or throws, then smaller sections can be intercut and linked, using grafting and a neat mattress-stitch. For example panels of Intarsia knit could be designed to link up with panels of, say, ribbing to provide one interesting solution to the problem of creating a larger-than-average piece.

Dedication and Patience

As a technique, Intarsia is relatively slow yet simple to operate. From my experience both as a teacher and user, a certain amount of patience and dedication is certainly required. This is especially so on the setting-up row when the knitter is confronted with a fearsome array of bobbins and colours, especially if the design is a complex one. However, the task becomes less daunting once a rhythm of work has been established. To me it is always worth persevering, but a small note of caution should be sounded. Taking into account the time which will be invested in a large and/or complex piece, it is vitally important that the design in question is well-conceived and sampled before starting the main work. Few things are so dishearten-

ing as spending many hours on a piece of work that turns out to be unsuccessful. Forward planning combined with a few samples and experiments will go a long way to ensuring that major projects end, not in tears, but success and pride in achievement.

Equipment and materials

Before beginning the discussion on how to transfer or adapt your designs into knitting, it is worth having a look at the equipment and materials involved.

Depending upon the individual make and model of your machine, you should be able to change the yarn-feed of the sinker-plate on your main carriage to an Intarsia-feed. Alternatively you may need a separate Intarsia carriage, which comes with its own tension-dial. You should check your machine's manual for the correct procedure.

Bobbins are required to wind the various yarns on. You will need a good supply of these as each individual section of the design requires a separate bobbin of colour. This can be roughly calculated beforehand by first counting the number of segments in the beginning row, and then looking for how many new colours are introduced at a later stage. Obviously some of the bobbins used at one point may not be needed for a particular section and can be employed later.

Bobbins can be purchased (see list of suppliers) or handmade from stout, non-bending card (see fig 110). Note that one of the gaps on the bobbin is very narrow. This allows yarn to be unwound in a controlled fashion as required. Balls of wool,

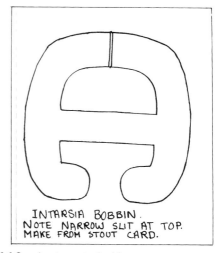

Fig 110. *An intarsia bobbin.*

although quicker to wind, tend to tangle easily and roll about. It is worth spending time preparing the bobbins, as time will be saved in the long run.

The wool-winder is extremely useful if you want to mix strands of different yarn together, perhaps various colours or a textured and a plain strand. A sizeable ball can be wound at one go and quantities transferred to a bobbin when necessary.

A good supply of weights is very important. The work in progress should have weights distributed across its full width. If this is not done, you will find frequent hitches occurring where loops do not knit off completely. This can happen especially with textured yarns. At worst the 'lay-in' yarn will jump the needles, resulting in a hole.

I find that the long lace weights supplied by various machine manufacturers are ideal for this purpose.

A tapestry-needle or latch-tool is a must for sewing-in the multitude of ends which the Intarsia technique generates.

Proportional graph paper, or, alternatively, paper for your charting device is also essential. Which you choose will depend on which method you choose to use. Another alternative is the Dawson's Grid© method.

Finally, you should have a good selection of yarns in various weights which can be mixed to a standard thickness, to maintain an even tension. Either single stranded or several ends of finer yarn can be bulked up to produce an equivalent weight.

First attempts

Experiment first before taking on a major new project. Work intuitively without graphs, but sketch out a few basic shapes as a starting point. Enjoy yourself but at the same time keep a record of notable successes and failures.

Start by setting up, for example, a simple stripe or chequerboard design, changing the widths, directions and colours. Try to find simple ways of altering the design by the way in which you work the knitting. Play around with mixed and solid colours; try flat colours without texture, then try putting more emphasis on textural changes with little or no variation in colour. Or you could try alternating thick and thin areas of knitting.

At this stage it doesn't matter if things go wrong or an idea doesn't work out. The whole point of experimenting is to find out what you can and can't get away with, and in this way you will gain valuable experience. Make notes and keep them with the samples you produce, and you will build up a useful store of reference material.

The following examples are provided to show you how you can evolve your own personal style. Time spent now can only help when the time comes to start designing for a complete piece. To help with your experiments several 'how to do it' samples are included.

Sample 1 (fig 111) – basic sample
This is a basic sample knitted on a standard punchcard machine (Brother) using a separate Intarsia carriage, but the same principles can be worked on a chunky machine or non-punchcard machine.

You will need five distinct colours or shades. I have used five shades ranging from white through three shades of grey to near-black. For this sample I used:

Colour A = White
Colour B = Light grey
Colour C = Mid grey
Colour D = Dark grey
Colour E = Near-black

Fig 111. *Sample 1. Intarsia method, knit facing, fine gauge.*

Use a tension appropriate to the yarn: I used the tension dial at No. 8.

1. Cast on with Colour A over 40 stitches.
Knit 6 rows using the main carriage.
Break off the yarn and set for Intarsia (see the instruction manual for your brand of machine). The needles are normally in the forward position to take the lay-in yarn.

2. Set up the following sequence of colours, from left to right:

14 needles . . . Colour E
 5 needles . . . Colour A
 4 needles . . . Colour D
12 needles . . . Colour C
 2 needles . . . Colour A
 3 needles . . . Colour E

Starting the knitting from the left, knit 8 rows using the Intarsia method.

3. The carriage should now be on the left. Using Colour E (which should be the leftmost bobbin) knit 2 rows across all the needles. This will produce a stripe of solid colour.

To vary the size and direction of a pattern section:
4. Return to the needle sequence of 2. Vary the widths of the strips by one to three stitches to the left and right of their last positions to form a zigzag stripe effect. Knit for 12 rows in this manner. Note that a movement greater than three stitches will start to produce cumbersome floats making that particular section of knitting less elastic than the surrounding areas.

Introducing a new bobbin of colour

5. The carriage should be on the left. Now introduce Colour B. Knit 2 rows across all the needles to form another stripe. Break off the yarn.

(A point of technique – always remember to hold down new ends of yarn for the setting-in row otherwise you will find that stitches may not knit off properly or not knit at all).

Reorganize the needle sequence as follows to let in another stripe in Colour B. Reading from left to right across the needle-bed, work:

7 needles . . . Colour E
7 needles . . . Colour B
5 needles . . . Colour A
4 needles . . . Colour D

Fig 112. *Sample 2. Intarsia method, purl facing, fine gauge, with a two-colour knit hem, and partial-knit triangular section.*

12 needles . . . Colour C
 2 needles . . . Colour A
 3 needles . . . Colour E

Knit 8 rows with this formation.

You will find that when new colours are introduced, the yarn ends that are hanging down should be uncrossed, as the original sequence has been

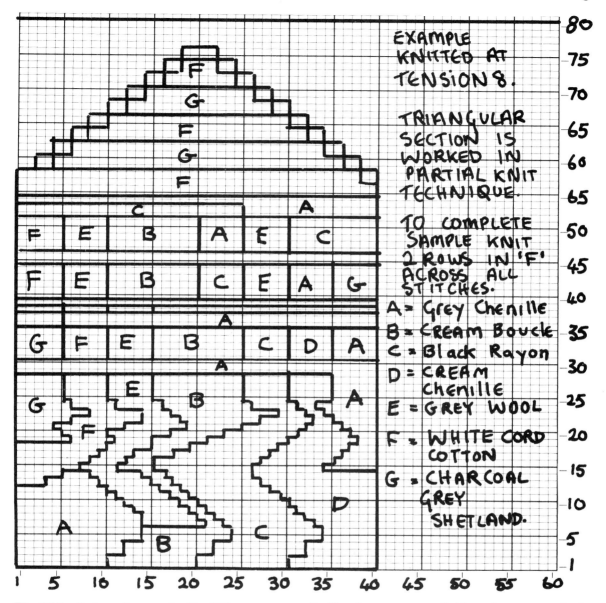

Handwritten notes on diagram:

EXAMPLE KNITTED AT TENSION 8.

TRIANGULAR SECTION IS WORKED IN PARTIAL KNIT TECHNIQUE.

TO COMPLETE SAMPLE KNIT 2 ROWS IN 'F' ACROSS ALL STITCHES.

A = Grey Chenille
B = CREAM Boucle
C = Black Rayon
D = CREAM Chenille
E = GREY WOOL
F = WHITE CORD COTTON
G = CHARCOAL GREY SHETLAND.

Fig 113. *Pattern diagram for Fig 112.*

broken. For example, Colour E will need to cross over Colour B in order to avoid a hole, and so on.

6. Knit 2 rows across all 40 stitches in Colour E.

7. Reset the colours on the needles as in the previous section. Knit 8 rows, but without crossing adjacent yarns.

This should produce a slit, which could be used as a design feature in a finished piece.

8. Knit 2 rows across all 40 stitches using a fresh bobbin of white (Colour A). Leave this attached on the left-hand side.

Eliminating certain colours from the design
9. Reorganize the needle sequence thus:

8 needles . . . Colour A
12 needles . . . Colour B
6 needles . . . Colour D
6 needles . . . Colour C
4 needles . . . Colour A
4 needles . . . Colour E

95

Knit 12 rows linking some areas by crossing adjacent yarns together and making slits between other colours. In my sample I kept the widths of the strips constant.

10. Working with the same sequence of colours, knit 8 rows, moving each colour one needle to the right on every row. Don't cross adjacent threads.

This should produce diagonal lines of small holes giving a decorative effect. If you want a smooth interlinked knit then the threads of adjacent colours should be crossed as in the next section where I have moved each colour one needle to the left on every row for 8 rows.

11. Finish the sample by knitting 6 rows of Colour E. Knit 2 rows of Colour A through the main carriage and cast off.

Sample 2 (fig 112) – development of zigzag stripes
Cast on 40 stitches at tension 8 in soft white cotton. Knit 6 rows.

Fig 114. *Fine gauge intarsia with applied tubes.*

Set for Intarsia and proceed as follows (the colours are my own selection – choose your own according to taste).

Colour A . . White corded cotton
Colour B . . Mohair and bouclé Black mix (two ends)
Colour C . . Pale Beige chenille
Colour D . . Near-black Shetland yarn
Colour E . . White and Cream fine bouclé (two ends)
Colour F . . Black synthetic chenille
Colour G . . Cream chenille
Colour H . . Two-strand Black rayon

Work from the graph in fig 113, crossing adjacent colours together. Intarsia can be decorated by the addition of narrow tubes of knitting (see fig 114).

Transferring the images into knitting

There are many ways of translating images into knitting. A graph-paper sheet can be constructed on which points are marked stitch for stitch and row for

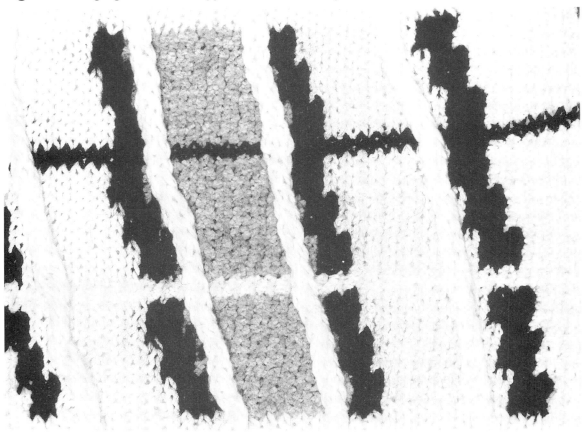

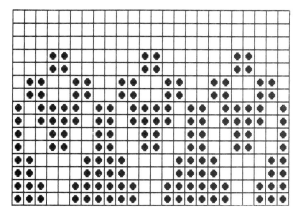
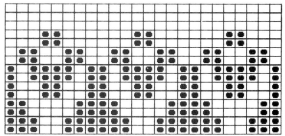

Fig 115. *Proportional versus non-proportional graph-paper.*

row. It is best to use proportional graph-paper as this is designed to allow for the fact that a stitch is not square. It ensures that a design drawn on the graph-paper knits up to the same proportions, *e.g.* a circle will remain a circle, rather than knitting up as an ellipse. The two diagrams (fig 115) show clearly how a design is transformed depending upon the size of the grid units.

Alternatively, a charting device can be used when working directly from a surface pattern design. This will give the correct proportion, full or half-scale. This method allows the knitter to concentrate on the creative aspects such as colour mixing and the various knitting techniques.

A third, more *ad hoc*, scheme is to work a direct interpretation from a squared-up paper rough of the design.

A fourth method is to use the Dawsons Grid© device.

Each method has its merits and pitfalls, and in all cases the knitter must make tension-squares for the main yarns to be used before beginning any work on the finished piece. This enables the right number of rows and stitches to be established (or the correct ruler to use if a charting-device is employed).

Before beginning to plan your graph it is important to remember that a graph is no more than a diagram. It does not form an exact equivalent of the actual size of a piece of knitting. The same graph can be used for knitting (by hand) extremely heavyweight yarn on very thick needles or ultrafine yarn on fine needles. Obviously, the finished pieces will vary greatly in size, but they will generally be of the same overall proportion.

Having decided upon the total number of rows and

stitches for each sample or section of the garment you wish to knit, make an outline of each of the shapes on graph-paper. Lightly pencil in the surface design, again in outline form, until you are satisfied with the proportions.

When this has been refined to your satisfaction, the outline can be stepped on the graph to represent

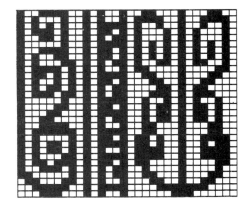

Fig 116. *Transforming a linear pattern to a blocked-in graph.*

Fig 117. *Outlined collar pattern prepared for a full-scale charting device.*

stitch-by-stitch changes. Fig 116 shows this process.

Where the drawn line divides one of the units it is up to you to decide which section you want the unit to be part of. In this situation I let the area of the largest proportion be the deciding factor.

At this stage I tend to work in black and white, although there is no reason why you shouldn't use colour.

A full-scale charting device is a most useful implement as the design does not then have to be scaled down. The method is as follows.

Draw the outline of your garment shape (full-scale)

on to a blank sheet of paper. Draw the actual design in outline on to this shape. Trace off the outline and then turn this sheet over if you want to avoid knitting a mirror image of your pattern. Tape the finished piece to a table top.

Lay the paper from the charter over this. Trace off the garment shape and design in line form, perhaps marking in the main colours. Continue now to work in the way you normally would, making tension squares in the main yarns in order to choose the correct stitch-rule and number of rows to be knitted.

I find that this is an extremely good (and quick) way of knitting intarsia. The knitter can see at a glance where the junctions between colours meet, and their exact needle positions (see fig 117).

Alternatively there is the Dawson Grid©, a device I first spotted at a trade show in 1988. It is a potentially invaluable aid for knitters working with both punch-card and electronic machines, and is also extremley useful in conjunction with intarsia technique.

It enables knitters to work directly from 'found' images, for example magazine pictures, photographs and traditional patterns, without having to draw them out as a preliminary step. The Dawson Grid© consists of a stout plastic sheet which has a grid of lines printed on the surface. A suitable image, such as a photo-graph, is attached to the reverse of the sheet with sticky tape. The image can then be copied point by point on to mylar sheet or graph-paper for two-colour pattern knitting, or read directly from the grid for intarsia work. An attached, movable plastic ruler makes reading the grid very easy.

The grid covers a frame of 70 stitches by 130 rows, but the width can be doubled by following the instructions provided. According to the manufac-turer, a piece of knitting worked in 4-ply on a standard gauge machine produces a picture of 138 stitches by 180 rows, giving an overall knitted size of around 46 cm (18 in) wide and 54 cm (21 in) long.

Of course, you are not limited to the actual size of the image being used. Some judicious reducing or enlarging on a photocopier of the original image makes the grid totally flexible.

In order to position the image correctly, and in proportion to the overall shape of the garment, you need to have a good idea of the number of stitches and rows required to knit (for example) the complete front of a sweater. I feel that a tension sample is best knitted first, and a calculation made of the number of rows and stitches for a given shape. The design can then be manipulated to fit in with this by uisng the photocopying method.

Alternatively, you can use the Dawson Grid© to work straight from your own drawings, and it can help you to bypass the time-consuming process of graphing out patterns, particularly for intarsia. Figs 118 and 119 show a design and part of a knitted sample produced using this method.

The following method is for the more adventurous. Knit tension squares in the main yarn. Decide on the number of rows and stitches reqired to knit a certain piece. Draw a grid of suitably-sized squares on the

Fig 118. *Knitted sample (chunky gauge) using the Dawson's Grid method.*

Fig 119. *Pattern for Fig 118 in linear form suitable for use with the Dawson's Grid©. Dimensions of the finished piece of knitting will vary depending upon tension. Knit the main pattern shapes using the intarsia method. Add fine linear details worked in Swiss darning, French knots and beading.*

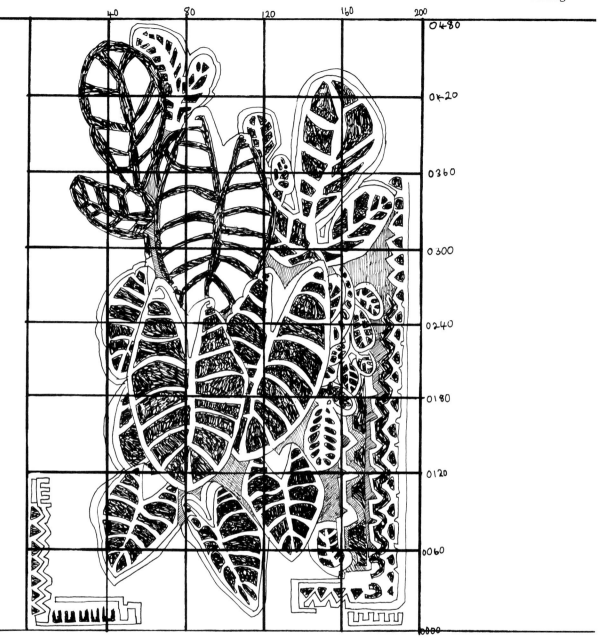

The grid is labelled along the top: 40, 80, 120, 160, 200

The grid is labelled along the right side: 0480, 0420, 0360, 0300, 0240, 0180, 0120, 0060, 0000

Fig 120. *Squared up pattern from which to work direct. Example shows a design for a large-scale panel. Each unit measures 15 × 15cm full-scale. Work drawing up to full-scale. Reverse image if asymmetrical. Mark out grid in equal size units. Knit tension square(s) in yarns and tension to be used in final piece. Calculate how many rows and stitches are equal to 1cm, then how many rows and stitches are needed to knit 1 unit of design grid. This will depend on tension. eg. Tension 6. 1cm = 2.667 sts and 3 rows. 1 unit (15 × 15cm) = 40 sts and 60 rows. Total number of stitches to be cast on = 40 sts × 5 = 200 sts. Total number of rows = 60 × 8 = 480 rows. More detail is achieved with fine tension/large scale.*

101

drawn image (as shown in fig 120) to give a rough idea where changes of colour occur. One square in the grid indicates the position of a particular portion of the design, and the number of rows and stitches necessary to knit it. Work directly from the appropriate tension square.

A final point for consideration is that when graphing an asymmetrical image, the rough (purl) side of the knitting, which faces you from the machine, will have the images running in the same direction as the graph, but the knit side will carry a mirror-image of the design. This should be born in mind if it is important to you that the image be a certain way round, if it contains letters or numbers, for example.

Sampling for Intarsia – Sources for Colour and Pattern

Start by choosing themes upon which to base your colour and pattern. You may decide to use ready-made design ideas, but to apply your own colour combinations to them.

Possible themes include Greek and Turkish folk-costumes of the nineteenth century; Victorian botanical illustrations (see *The World Of Kew* by Ronald King); Ancient Egyptian imagery; embroideries, such as Spanish Blackwork of the sixteenth century; English Jacobean bedcovers; English Tudor caps; children's drawings and paintings; or canal boat decoration.

Additional ideas for colour could derive from photographs of carnivals, fairgrounds, exotic birds and fish or tropical flowering plants.

Whatever theme you decide to explore, I suggest you choose fairly clear, bold pictorial or geometric images in which line and blocked-in shapes are the main ingredients, and the main colours total no more than five or six to begin with (see figs 121 and 122). You should also look at the work of painters and artists generally, especially those of the late nineteenth and twentieth centuries. Note how they made effective use of shape and colour. Look at work by Matisse, Derain, Dufy, Bonnard and Vuillard.

Sources of design ideas are everywhere once you get into the habit of looking for them, but avoid simply copying other designers' ideas – it's much better to evolve your own!

Fig 121. *Intarsia design based on window patterns, using hand-knit yarns on a chunky gauge machine.*

Mixing yarns

If you are at this stage you should have done one of two things. Either you have designed an image of your own and you are at the stage of working out suitable colours and yarns, or you are using an image taken from a magazine or some similar source and you want to develop your own ideas about colour and texture, using this image as a basis. Figs 123–125 show three design ideas I have been working on for the bodice of an intarsia jacket.

Don't worry if you usually work with a suggested colour-range from a bought pattern. This is a chance to break out and establish your own personal style in colour and yarn combinations.

Fig 122. *A more detailed version of Fig 121. Swiss darning is used to add points of interest to the design.*

Fig 123. *Design ideas for a shaped intarsia bodice.*

Fig 124. *as Fig 123.*

Concerning choice of yarns, I suggest that if you are considering knitting a fair amount of intarsia work that you should always be on the look-out for suitable materials. This is the one machine-knit technique in which very small amounts of yarn, perhaps saved from other projects, can be used to advantage.

It is a good plan to buy up small balls of wool and other suitable threads when the opportunity arises (for example yarns meant for hand-knitting, but of a suitable weight for either the fine or chunky gauge machine).

Try to organize a suitable storage system that allows you to see the variety of yarns at a glance. I have a large collection of old sweet-jars which make handy containers for all the very small balls of wool, sorted by colour – reds in one jar, greens and blues in another. It is important that you can easily see all the colours available in order to be able to refer quickly to them when sampling.

You should bear in mind that it is not possible to alter the tension midway through a row, and there-

Fig 125. *as Fig 123.*

fore you should ensure that the yarns used in that row are compatible in this respect. If you aren't careful about this, the finished piece may well be distorted or fail to hang correctly, particularly if many colour changes occur in each row.

As well as compatible tension settings, weight and density must both be matched on any one particular piece. To illustrate what I mean by density, consider a mohair yarn and a fine, smooth cotton yarn both knitted at Tension 8. The mohair will fill out the knitted surface much more so than the cotton, and can be said to have a greater density than the cotton. The word 'cover' is sometimes employed in the same context.

If problems of badly matched density arise, a solution could be to add other strands of yarn to the cotton, which may provide a better coverage. Try out a few small strip samples so that you can compare options.

It is also worth perfecting your technique with yarns that are relatively easy to handle (smooth wools, cottons, and silks, for example). Gradually build up to knitting intarsia with textured and multi-stranded yarns. This can produce subtle variations within a narrow colour range depending upon the proportion of one colour to another within the mix.

As an example, combine one thick strand of blue with one thin strand of green. This will knit up to a predominantly blue colour with a hint of green. Similarly, the same blue combined with a fine red strand will produce a blue tinged with red. By varying the respective thicknesses of the two yarns, a range of shades between the two extremes can be produced.

More samples

For your first samples I suggest a limit of about five or six colour variations. Begin by making several yarn fringes consisting of half a dozen ends of yarn that echo the colours in your chosen source material. Try to find yarn that, when knitted, will suggest a similar texture. Attempt various solutions using different yarns of the same weight, in varying qualities and colours.

You may for instance decide that the design needs to be knitted in completely smooth yarns, particularly if the design is hard-edged and geometric. Subtle changes can be implemented by using smooth wools, cottons and silks of the same weight, all having slightly differing reflective qualities. Silk, being an expensive yarn, could be used in small quantities in a highlighting capacity.

Choose one particular fringe that appeals to you. You can next experiment with colour or textural balance by wrapping the same group of yarns around several stout pieces of card, but varying the proportions from card to card. Repeat the same colour in different places so you can see the effect it has on various neighbouring colours.

I have chosen as my theme colours found in a midsummer garden, and have used photos, seed catalogues, real plants and botanical illustrations as source material. If you would like to develop this theme for yourself, some additional points of reference could be magazine cuttings, photos and sketches of gardens, a visit to a botanical garden (take a camera and/or crayons and a sketch-book to note down colours), or the grounds of a country house.

The yarns selected are intended to evoke some of the surface qualities of the various flowers and leaves to be found in the garden. At the time I made my samples, most of the flowers were shades of red varying from pink to crimson, scarlet and magenta.

Foliage contributed silvery-grey tones and leaf-greens, while rich, dark browns derive from the soil, and woody shades from bark and fencing.

A good approach is to make a layout of all the colours you can see. If you have followed the advice in the introductory chapter, you will have a supply of coloured paper and fabric, magazine clippings and so on. Sort out some relevant shades and tones from

Fig 126. *Design sheet showing a series of ideas for an evening sweater using the intarsia method. Suggested yarns: Silks, cottons and rayons.*

this material, tear it into various sized pieces and proceed to make a collage.

Vary the size of the bits and play around with them, trying different combinations of colours on differing areas. You can stick the pieces down when you are happy with the arrangement, and either leave it as it is or work on it some more using other media.

Coloured chalk will give a rough, textured appearance; pencil will give a metallic sheen, and wax crayon will give a glossy effect. This sort of thing may seem like child's play, but no professional designer embarks on a new project without preliminary paperwork, and the method just described is frequently employed by both knit and weave designers as a means of bridging the gap between an initial idea and its realization as a finished piece.

Choose several groups of five or six colours. Copy these combinations into a notebook (A6 size is probably best) as splodges or bands of adjacent colours.

Prior to applying colour and texture to any given design, I like to work out some of my ideas for combinations and proportions of yarn-mixes on a 'chequerboard' sample. Not only can these samples act as possible colour palettes for future design, but they are also very useful for comparing the surface qualities that the various yarns acquire when knitted up.

Such a sample will be a useful guide to how the tension setting affects the different yarns you wish to use. The square format will immediately show up any problems in this department since if one yarn-type gives a larger (or smaller) than normal stitch, its square will tend to bulge and/or distort the lines of the chequerboard. The sample will also give information about comparative yarn coverage.

For the professional designer the chequerboard samples have an additional purpose. If a retailer is thinking of purchasing a number of garments, it is likely that the buyer will want to see alternative colourways to the sample shown. It is neither economical nor necessary to produce a range of complete samples in different colourways, and the squared colour samples serve the purpose admirably.

A sample containing between 12 and 16 units is about right for the purpose. For the fine-gauge machine I would suggest that each unit be 10 stitches by 12 rows – 4 units up and 4 units across. For the chunky-gauge, 5 or 6 stitches by 7 or 8 rows is better.

Use a gauge of machine and a tension which suits the materials with which you intend to work. You could start the chequered samples by choosing any two distinctly opposing colours from one of the six colour ranges.

Knit up one complete 4 by 4 sample. For my sample I used Shocking Pink and Jade Green in equal proportions. It may be that you decide that the Jade Green is right for the design but you would prefer a slightly more subdued pink for Colour B. Refer back to the chosen group of six colours. I replaced the Shocking Pink with a much more orangey-pink colour.

There are many ways to develop the chequerboard. For example, assume a sample square using 8 units each of Colours A and B. First, take Colour A and replace some of the eight units with other colours which are either contained within the colour fringes or the wrappings which I originally suggested you make. My diagram shows:

Colour A remaining in 4 squares, and also
8 units of Colour B
2 units of Colour C
1 unit of Colour D
1 unit of Colour E

Again, for example, Colour A could be nearly half of the design and be apportioned 7 out of the 16 units. Colours B, C and D are less important and could be assigned 3, 3, and 2 units respectively. Colour E is to be used sparingly, and so could be given 1 unit only. This last colour could be used as the highlight colour in the finished piece – maybe the one very light colour in a mainly dark combination.

Try, then, arranging the various colours within the 16-unit sample, putting colours next to one another as you intend them to be in the final design. You could perhaps work this out approximately using coloured pencils, prior to the actual knitting, or use some of the collected samples of colour in your general colour reference file.

The 16-unit sample gives you the opportunity to place the same colour against several other colours in the range, and to see how they react together. Maybe Colour A complements Colour C perfectly, but when placed next to Colour E, takes on a dull appearance.

The sampler also acts as a guide to the amount or proportion of each colour needed to work a particular design.

By this stage you will have looked at possible colour combinations. Now try juggling various yarn qualities – perhaps substituting all the green (Colour B) with, say, cottons or chenilles, or perhaps rayon – to try out various types of knitted surfaces – still matching tensions and density.

How the chequerboard unit is developed now depends very much on how many different colours you need, or wish to use, in the finished design. New sample pieces could be developed putting the emphasis on another colour, and rearranging the subsidiary colours in different ways. Try out ideas and observe the changes rather than worrying too much about what will happen if you do a certain procedure.

For example – I found that a rich dark brown, which was not originally included in my range, both echoed the source material and added depth to the pinks and greens. At a later point I tried substituting colours and added an intense purple-blue (derived from Delphinium flowers) and an ochre which reflected the centre of another flower.

The accumulated odd balls of yarn from previous projects really came into their own, giving me the opportunity to try all sorts of ideas without having to go and buy large quantities, which I might not eventually have used.

It is not necessary to knit each variation – if you have paints, coloured pencils or coloured papers to hand. Try working out some new concepts on paper, and only re-knit the most successful.

You should now have a colourful selection of

samples, both knitted and worked in and/or on paper. Think of them as a variety of colour palettes from which to choose.

Virtues of these chequered samples include their small size, and the fact that they are quick to produce, so it doesn't matter much if some are not a success. Take a failed idea as a starting point for the next one. These experiments will help to put some structure into the way that you organize your colours.

If you have an ear for music, you will know that combinations of notes can be harmonious or discordant – colours work together in a similar way. Bright, clashing colour combinations are often referred to as 'loud' or 'discordant'. Or we talk about 'muted tones' in a design. One might deliberately choose to put bright, contrasting colours together for effect – making the colours work against each other. A bright,

vigorous pink will glow even more in a setting of green shades. A generally soft, low-key design can often benefit from small, bright highlights.

Learn to orchestrate colour by trying out different relationships and altering proportions within a tight group of about half a dozen hues. You could perhaps even use a favourite piece of music to inspire a choice of colours, and apply the combinaton to a design.

The final step is to apply colour to pattern. The same pattern can be tried in varying combinations of colour, changing the emphasis to a brighter, lighter, or darker design.

Work through some small samples before applying yourself to a finished garment. Fig 126 shows a series of potential ideas for an evening sweater knitted in the intarsia technique.

CHAPTER 5
Partial knitting as a decorative technique

Short row, or partial knitting, can be used to produce a limited range of offset stripe patterns, single and linked geometric shapes on patterned backgrounds, or bold, clearly defined shapes set against a plain ground.

Plain knitting, two-colour pattern method, ribbing and intarsia can all be combined. Chapter 8 looks at the latter possibilities in greater depth.

Partial knitting comes into its own where areas of plain and patterned knitting are combined (no other method can produce these results), or where the overall shaping of a section is arrived at by the partial knit method, and is an integral part of the design, be it plain or patterned knit (see figs 129 and 130).

It is feasible to create beautifully shaped sections of knitting using this method, in which the surface patterns combine closely with the overall shape of the piece.

To this end I have included directions on how to get the most out of short-row shaping at a fairly early stage in the chapter. This is followed by a look at the different types of patterning possible, which in turn can be worked within various overall shapes.

The range of possible imagery is limited by two main factors. First, the more intricate a shape is, the more time it takes to knit, and other methods (*e.g.* intarsia) may be more suitable. Second, some shapes are just impractical, if not impossible, to knit using this method.

You should see from a basic understanding of partial knitting that at least one needle must be put into holding position (or E position on some models)

Fig 129. *Pleated collar using the partial knit method.*

on alternate rows if a flat, completely linked surface is to be achieved.

The graph in Fig 131a demonstrates a simple shape that would work successfully assuming a two-colour pattern, where Colour A is the first colour to be knitted.

■ = Colour A
□ = Colour B

Starting from the bottom right-hand corner, the written instructions to this graph would be:

1. Knit 2 rows in Colour A.
2. Carriage on the right.
3. Push 1 needle into HP on the left-hand side, and set the carriage to partial knit.
4. Knit 2 rows.
5. Push another needle into HP on the left.
6. Knit 2 rows.
7. Continue in this manner until all needles are in HP.

Transfer the carriage to the left-hand side without knitting. Push the first needle (that closest to the carriage) down into WP and knit two rows. Continue pushing needles back into WP until rows 21 and 22 where all needles are knitted in colour B.

The main point to notice is that short-row knitting is worked in pairs of rows, where at least one stitch per two rows is put into HP at the opposite end to the carriage.

Technically, any number of stitches per group can be put into HP, although the final shape of the image to be knitted will influence the choice.

The reason for needing at least one new needle in HP on alternate rows is to allow for the yarn to be looped under the last needle in HP. This avoids loops building up or a gap forming. For example, knitting four rows without adding to the needles already in HP would result in two loops on the last needle in HP. Knitting six rows would result in a build-up of three loops, and so on. Of course, it is not obligatory to make a loop if for some reason you want to leave a gap between the sections. As will be seen in Chapter 6 on slitted knitting, this variation of technique can be used decoratively.

Following on from this, the next two graphs (figs 131 b and c) demonstrate shapes that are *not* suitable for this method, if gaps are to be avoided. 131b is 5 stitches wide and 20 rows deep. The aim is to knit a rectangle divided evenly into two triangular shapes, the angle between the two sections A and B being particularly steep. The graph shows the only way in

Fig 130. *Dress, using a combination of partial knit, plain and patterned knitting.*

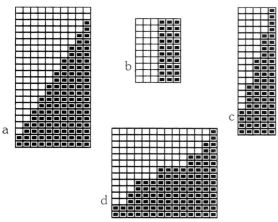

Fig 131a. *Successful regular shape for partial knit.*
Fig 131b. *Unsuitable shapes for partial knit.*
Fig 131c. *Unsuitable shapes for partial knit.*
Fig 131d. *Successful irregular shape for partial knit.*

which this could be achieved, stitch for stitch and row by row.

However, it can be seen that in knitting this shape, there would either be two loops around the last needle in HP, or a gap (if the yarn is not wound around this needle) as it takes four rows to knit each step.

A similar shape, using either 10 stitches by 20 rows, or 5 stitches by 10 rows, could be knitted using partial-knit however; only 2 rows are then needed in between steps. Try some graphs of your own if you are unsure how this works.

Fig 131b and c could quite easily be knitted using the intarsia method, though, as this is knitted one full row at a time (see Chapter 4).

Graph 131b is also impossible to knit by the short-row method unless a gap of ten rows is required. If this were to be knitted, looping yarn under the last needle in HP, five loops would result. Or if the yarn were not looped around this needle, then a slit would arise between sections A and B. Again the intarsia method would overcome the problem.

Fig 131d shows that it is possible to knit irregular geometric shapes as long as you work on the principle of putting at least one extra needle into HP every two rows.

This is the one technique where I feel you must use a graph, and work the shapes out thoroughly before knitting. You therefore need to know how many rows and stitches make up the area to be designed on, which in turn means the production of a tension-square of the yarn you intend using.

I would not advocate using the charting device for decorative short-row knitting as you cannot tell in advance whether any of the problems mentioned will surface. Instead, use a graph at an early stage of designing in order to pre-empt difficulties.

If you find it easier to work from written instructions for partial knit, a written pattern follows for the last graph, fig 131d. I would, however, suggest that you always make a graph first. Try to lay out the instructions in a format that is easy to read quickly. For example: Casting on 14 stitches in Colour A, commence knitting with the carriage on the right-hand side. Knit 2 rows across all stitches.

Please remember, as always, that the direction of the shapes on the graph is as it will be on the purl face of the knitting.

Commence knitting with the carriage on the right. Follow the arrows in the left-hand column.

Carr. Direction	Row Counter	Directions
← →	000–002	Knit. Push First 2 needles into HP on left.
← →	002–004	Knit. Push 1 needle into HP on left.
← →	004–006	Knit. Push 3 needles into HP on left.
← →	006–008	Knit. Push 4 needles into HP on left.
← →	008–010	Knit. Push 2 needles into HP on left.
← →	010–012	Knit. Push 1 needle into HP on left.
← →	012–014	Knit. (12 rows in total) Transfer Carriage to left. Thread up Colour B. Reset row-counter using the transfer tool. Push into WP first 2 needles on left.
⇄	000–002	Knit. Push into WP 1 needle on left.
⇄	002–004	Knit. Push into WP 3 needles on left.
⇄	004–006	Knit. Push into WP 4 needles on left.
⇄	006–008	Knit. Push into WP 2 needles on left.
⇄	008–010	Knit. Push into WP 1 needle on left
⇄	010–012	Knit. (12 rows in total)

This completes the graph sequence.

A final introductory word on this method: before trying to design specific shapes, it is worth noting that on a sample, say, 40 stitches wide, it will only take 8 rows to knit a diagonal where 10 stitches are put into HP on every alternate row (until all stitches are in HP).

At the other end of the scale, and working on the same 40 stitches, putting 1 stitch into HP on every alternate row until all needles are in HP, the steepest part of the slope would be 80 rows in depth. That is, the shallower the angle between Section A and Section B over any given number of stitches, the fewer rows are needed to make the shape.

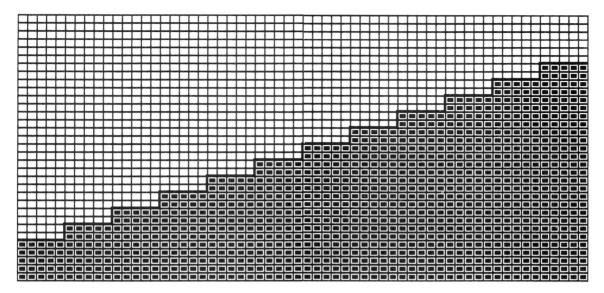

Fig 132. *Pattern graph for Sample 1 (partial knitting), 60 stitches wide. Commence knitting from the bottom left-hand corner. Partial knit sections use groups of 5 needles in HP every alternate row.*

Basic Experiments in Partial Knitting using Plain Knitting

In this section I will deal with the three main ways of working with Partial Knitting for decorative knitting:

Group 1. Wedge and triangular-shaped patterns in contrasting colours or yarns.
Group 2. Stripe patterns.
Group 3. Shaped sections of knitting that also incorporate stripes, wedges and colour changes.

The following directions can be worked on almost any machine, chunky or fine-gauge, provided that you have a Partial Knit setting. You will *not* need a pattern card.

Group 1 – Samples
Sample 1 (fig 132) – basic pattern
Use two yarns of equal weight in Colour A and Colour B at a suitable tension. The listed details are from my own sample.

Yarn   – 2-ply Shetland sweater weight
Tension – 8 (normal-gauge machine)
Machine – Jones KH-830
Colours – A = Off-white
             B = Charcoal

Fig 133. *Bands of partial knit using groups of 5, 4 then 3 needles pushed into HP on alternate rows over 60 stitches. Use Fig 132 as a staring point.*

Use weights throughout, particularly around the area where HP and WP needles are adjacent. This helps to stop a bunch-up of knitted rows and the consequent failure to knit off properly.

You may have to improvise. The idea is to make sure that some downward tension is applied to all the stitches on the needles, since otherwise the needle latches can't function properly. You will almost certainly find this easier to arrange if the cast-on comb (Brother machines) is removed and replaced with individual weights spaced along the knitting, once the first few rows are completed. If you don't do this, you may find that the comb tangles with the carriage when knitting steep angles.

Sample 2 (fig 134) – varying the angles
This next sample gives details on ways of achieving a variety of angles between two sections using non-repetitive groupings of needles in HP. Again choose two contrasting colours of yarn. Cast on 60 stitches.

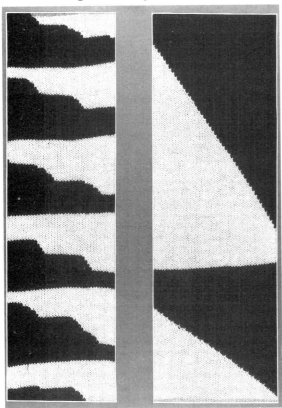

Fig 134. *Sample showing a range of angles between partial knit sections, achieved by various groupings of needles put into HP over alternate rows.*

The sample can now be developed trying various groupings of needles. Again work in pairs of rows, reversing the instructions when knitting the second section. It works as follows:

If, for example, you have had 4 needles in HP on the right, and 26 needles in WP when knitting in Colour A, the same four needles must be returned to WP when knitting in Colour B, and the 26 needles will be in HP.

Suggested groupings for the stocking stitch sampler are:
(knit 6 rows in between each section).

a)   10, 1, 9, 2, 8, 3, 7, 4, 6, 5, 5
b)   10, 1, 2, 9, 3, 4, 8, 5, 6, 7, 5
c)   10, 1, 2, 3, 4, 9, 5, 6, 7, 8, 5

Another sample could worked dividing the groups into sub-sections which are then repeated three times. Again knit 6 rows between each section. Cast on 48 sts.

a)   10, 3, 2, 1   10, 3, 2, 1   10, 3, 2, 1
b)   12, 2, 1, 1   12, 2, 1, 1   12, 2, 1, 1
c)   3, 2, 1, 10   3, 2, 1, 10   3, 2, 1, 10
d)   1, 1, 1, 13   1, 1, 1, 13   1, 1, 1, 13
e)   10, 3, 2, 1   12, 2, 1, 1   3, 2, 1, 10
f)   1, 1, 2, 12   12, 2, 1, 1   1, 2, 3, 10

Group 2 – Samples
The next set of samples look at ways in which stripes can be created within the wedge-shaped section shown in the previous examples. The method (working section by section) is also as before.

I have limited myself to working tonally, using a main light and dark colour with subtle variations.

Samples 3 and 4 (figs 135, 136 and 137) – combining wedges and stripes
This shows a simple wedge and strip pattern in graph form, with five main sections. The illustrations give an idea of how it could look knitted in various qualities of yarn, ranging from pure new wools to slub cottons and fancy glitter yarns. Stockists of such yarns include Brockwell Wools, King Kole and Yeoman Yarns.

The scalloped edge on all the samples is knitted as follows:
1. Thread up Colour E. Set the carriage for plain knit. Knit 2 rows.
2. Reset the carriage for HP. Push every 4th needle (counting from the left edge) into HP in the

Right **Fig 135.** *Pattern graph in 5 sections.*

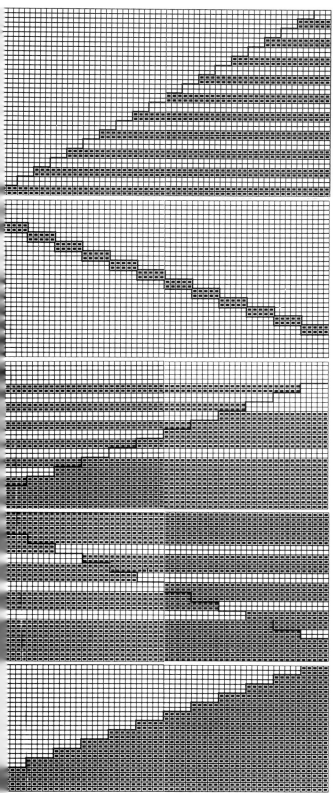

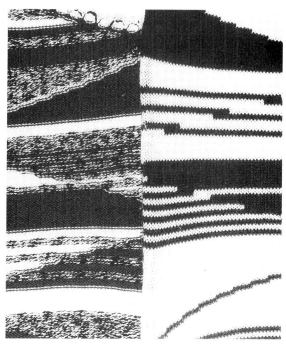

Fig 136. *Sample 3 (partial knit) worked from Fig 135.*

Fig 137. *Sample 4 (partial knit). An alternative version knitted from Fig 135 in fancy yarns.*

following way; WWWH – WWWH – etc, where W is working position and H is holding position.

3. Make sure that the knitting is weighted at regular close intervals. Knit 4 rows across the needles in this setting.

4. Set the carriage for plain knit. Knit 1 row in Colour C, followed by 1 row in Colour E.

5. Cast off loosely. The result should be a scalloped edge.

It is possible to develop quite an intricate range of wedge and triangular-shaped segments using partial knitting.

The exercises in this section are designed to help you understand their construction, and you can then practise knitting a collection of shapes in plain knit using a good quality, smooth-textured, easy to knit yarn (instructions to follow). Once you feel confident at this level you will then find it much easier to apply various types of surface decoration in whichever technique you choose.

Of course it is possible to regard each individually shaped piece as a unit of repeat that could also be developed to form a larger area of pattern either by linking the units together as a continuous shaped surface during the knitting process, or by applying them to a background of knitting or other fabric.

Group 3 – samples

Each of the following samples (figs 138 and 139) uses two or three contrasting yarns of similar weight. They can all be made on any gauge machine, as long as a partial-knit setting is available.

Sample 5 (fig 138, bottom)

1. Cast on 40 stitches at a suitable tension. Begin knitting with the carriage on the right, and the machine set for partial-knit.

2. Knit 2 rows in Colour A, then push 2 needles into HP on the left, on every alternate row, until all needles are in HP.

3. Change to Colour B. Push back into WP (use the transfer-tool) a pair of adjacent needles on every alternate row until all needles are returned to WP. Knit 2 complete rows.

4. Repeat steps 1, 2 and 3 three times, producing three main segments A, B and C.

Sample 6 (fig 138, middle)

This sample develops the idea used in Sample 5 by starting the second segment, B from the left-hand side instead of the right. Segments A and C still start from the right.

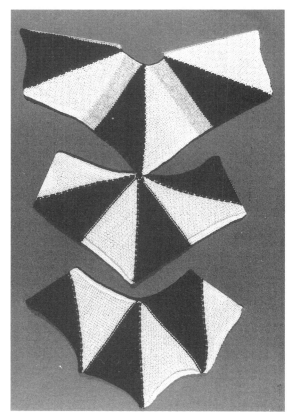

Fig 138. *Examples of various shaped sections using the partial knit technique.*

Note that in order to move an empty carriage from one end of the needle-bed to the other across threaded-up needles, it is possible on most makes of machines to use the Slip setting. This will not disturb the stitches already on the needles. Do not use this method on a Brother machine when there are needles in the forward patterning position. The knitting will fall off!

Sample 7 (fig 138, top)

Ten rows of plain, straight knitting have been introduced before each main section of partial knitting. In this sample, all the partial-knit sections commence from the right-hand side.

Call the straight segment 'D'. A, B and C are as in Sample 5.

Cast on 40 stitches. Knit as follows:

1. Segment D.

2. Segment A. Start from right-hand side (RHS).

3. Segment D.

4. Segment B. Start from RHS.
5. Segment D.
6. Segment C. Start from RHS.
7. Segment D.
End of sequence.

Sample 8 (fig 139, top)
This sample follows the same basic method as Sample 7, but reverses the starting point of one of the partial-knit sections.

Cast on 40 stitches. Knit as follows:

1. Segment D.
2. Segment A. Start from RHS.
3. Segment D.
4. Segment B. Start from LHS.
5. Segment D.
6. Segment C. Start from RHS.
7. Segment D.
End of sequence.

Sample 9 (fig 139, middle)
This sample examines one way of varying the amount of needles put into Hold Position (HP) groups.

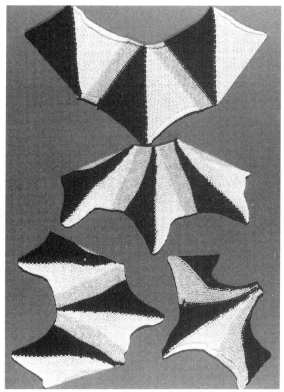

Fig 139. *More complex shaped sections exploiting the partial knit technique.*

1. Cast on 40 stitches.
2. Begin with carriage on RHS. Knit 10 rows in Colour C.
3. Change to Colour A, and set for partial-knit.
4. Put 5 needles on LHS into HP on every alternate row. Do this 5 times (should take 10 rows, and leave 25 needles in HP).
5. Put 1 needle on LHS into HP every alternate row. Do this 15 times. This should leave 40 needles in HP.

(The complete procedure from 4 to 5 inclusive should have taken 10 + 30 rows, a total of 40 rows).

6. Using Colour B, reverse the process for 4 and 5 until all working needles are returned to WP. This should take another 40 rows.
7. Repeat this entire unit (2 to 6) 3 times, commencing each section of partial knitting from the RHS.

Sample 10 (fig 139, bottom)
This sample is knitted as Sample 9, except that each consecutive partial-knit segment starts from the side opposite the previous one.

Using these samples as information, try out some shapes of your own devising. If you compare, for example, Sample 5 with Sample 9, the overall shape of the unit is dependent upon:

1. The number of needles per group being put into HP at any one time.
2. The starting point of the knitting, *i.e.* all pieces starting on the left or right, or some pieces starting on the left and some on the right (this may be just alternate sides, or a more complex repeat).

The next step is to make use of decorated shaped units. An easy exercise to try out first is to use patterned knitting as a dividing band between shapes rather than by applying it to the shapes themselves.

Pattern-card knitting combined with partial-knit

The simplest method of introducing pattern-card knit into areas of partial-knit is in straight sections. You do not need any extra technical knowledge for this as you will already have practised using the pattern card and two-colour knitting. This method is examined in greater detail, however, in Chapter 8.

I suggest using a relatively small scale pattern and

experimenting with different textures of yarn in light and dark tones.

Sample 11 (fig 140, top)
1. Cast on 40 stitches using 2 contrasting colours, using a suitable tension.
2. Commence with the carriage on the LHS. Knit 10 rows of 2-colour pattern (my example is chequerboard).
3. Push 5 needles at opposite end to carriage into HP.
4. Knit to the left and to the right, looping either one or both yarns under the last needle in HP before the return row.

5. Continue in this manner until all needles are in HP.
6. Knit 2 rows of plain knitting, using the 2nd row to pre-set the needles for the next patterned section.
7. Repeat these sections as many times as required.

My sample has six repeats, finishing with 10 rows of patterned knit over all 40 stitches. Note that if you require a change of pattern-card then this should be done prior to knitting the two plain rows.

Sample 12 (fig 140, bottom)
This sample avoids a break in the patterning between segments by missing out the two plain-knit rows. The instructions are the same as Sample 11 until the point

Fig 140. *Patterned, shaped sections knitted in contrasting yarns.*

Fig 141. *Single shaped unit using plain and patterned knitting.*

Fig 142. *A composite sample repeating the unit pictured in Fig 141 varying textures and tonal balance. A possible idea for an exotic collar.*

where all needles have been put into HP and the carriage is on the left.

1. Break off the yarn. Move the carriage (still in HP) across the needles in HP to the right.
2. Manually push all the working needles back into WP. Set for slip and move the carriage from right to left. The needles will be set for patterned knitting.
3. Reset the carriage for HP and patterned knitting. Thread up yarns A and B and repeat the sequence as many times as required.

The pattern card can be changed to suit, as can the colours and yarns. Try experimenting. Fig 140 also shows a similar section worked in a black mohair yarn (Texere Yarns) and a cotton mix (Bramwell). See figs 141 and 142, too, where plain and patterned rows have been worked together in one sample.

Sample 13 (fig 143)
This sample uses the scalloped edge technique as a way of dividing partial knit sections. Choose five yarns of approximately the same weight (this sample is knitted in Yeoman yarns):

Cream chenille (A)
Silver Butterfly quality (B)
Black chenille (C)
Black/multi Butterfly quality (D)
White wool (4-ply) (E)

1. With the carriage on the left, cast on 60 stitches.
2. Knit 6 rows (A) at tension 8, ending up with the carriage on the RHS.
3. Knit 4 rows of each of the first 4 qualities, at the same time pushing 3 needles into HP every alternate row until 36 needles are in HP.
4. Thread up (E). Set carriage for plain-knit. Knit 2 rows.
5. Reset carriage for HP. Counting from LHS, push out every 4th needle into HP. Weight the knitting at regular intervals. Knit 4 rows with the needles in this position.
6. Reset carriage for plain-knit. Knit 1 row (C), then 1 row (E).
7. Push 36 needles on LHS into HP, and then return the first 3 needles of this group (before you knit anything) to WP. Knit 2 rows, working the colour sequence in reverse of the 1st section. Continue until all needles are back in WP. End with 2 complete rows of (A).
8. Repeat the sequence from 3 to 7 as many times as you wish.

Fig 143. *Partial knit sections divided by the scalloped-edge technique.*

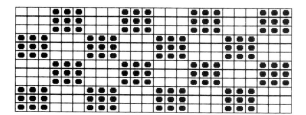

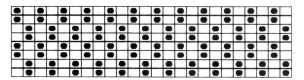

Fig 144. *Pattern graphs for the chequerboard and birdseye designs.*

Variations again depend upon changes of yarns, the number of rows in any particular colour, and the number of needles in HP. It is essential to keep clear records of these processes.

When using the pattern-card and partial knitting I have found that in some cases it is necessary to wind both yarns A and B under the last needle in HP before the return row.

It seems to depend on the type of yarn being used. Lightweight yarns, such as synthetic chenille, when used against a more solid yarn, such as cotton, have a tendency to catch on the gate-pegs if not wound under the last needle in HP as well, particularly if such a yarn is in the second yarn-feed.

I have found that if the yarns used are both identical wool or cotton then only one yarn (the main one) needs to be wound under this last needle. It is a situation with no hard and fast rule, and you will need to experiment. The type of machine you are using will also have some bearing on this.

The only problem with winding both yarns is that by the time the second section is being knitted, an extra four loops will be on the particular needle.

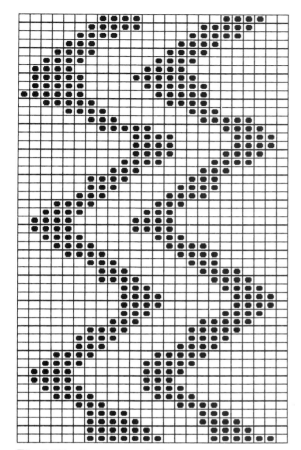

Fig 145. *Pattern graph for zigzag design.*

An alternative method is to knit two rows of plain knitting before knitting the second section. I prefer to do this as it gives a good clean edge on double-over sections.

Another problem which needs solving is how best to deal with the joining rows beteen the edge of one pattern using Partial Knit and another. There are several solutions.

The difficulty occurs after Section A has been knitted. Needles for Section B are pushed back into WP but cannot be automatically set for the correct row of pattern knit until one row has been knitted. It is possible to select the needles by hand, sorting them into positions A and B prior to knitting each pair of rows on Brother machines.

This is not too difficult if you are knitting a simple, regular chequerboard, stripe or some similar geometric design. If, however, it is a more complex and irregular pattern, then the hand-selection has to be worked from a graph, and this can be time-consum-

ing. If you just push all the needles back to WP and knit, a generally untidy join will be the result.

The other solution is this; after Section A has been knitted, knit either one or two rows between each section in the main colour for the next section. There is no real need then to hand-select the pattern needles.

Miscellaneous samples

Samples 14 and 15 introduce a range of variously textured yarns – Tussah Silk, Rayon, Cotton, Chenille and Lurex – from Texere Yarns, and work through other interpretations of instructions already given (see figs 146).

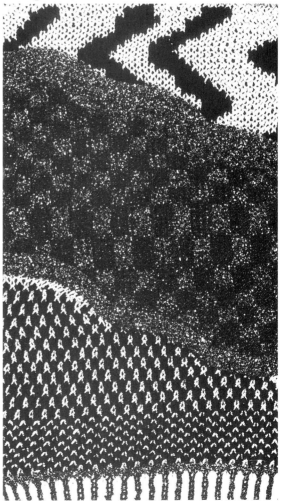

Fig 146. *Partial knit sample in strongly contrasting textures.*

119

Fig 147. *Partial knit sample introducing the triangular flap.*

Finally sample 16 deals with with ways of using the shaped hem in a decorative manner. The same method can be used for making triangular flaps to insert into an area of pattern (fig 147). To make a shaped hem:

1. Cancel the patterned knitting buttons and HP.
2. Knit 2 rows in black yarn, using the second row to preset the needles for the pattern.
3. Thread up feed A as white, feed B as black. Set the carriage for partial knitting and the pattern card on lock.
4. The carriage should be on the LHS of the needle-bed. Push 4 needles into HP on RHS. Knit to the right.
5. Push 4 needles on LHS into HP and knit to the left.
6. Continue in this manner until all but the centre eight needles are in HP.

For a Brother machine:

1. Push 4 needles on RHS back into WP. Hand-select the pattern position of these 4 needles. Knit to the right.
2. Push 4 needles on LHS back to WP. Manually set for pattern and knit to the left.
3. Continue in this manner until all needles are in WP.

For a Knitmaster machine:
As it is not possible to view the needle selection, as is the case on the Brother machine, it is easier to knit two rows of plain-knit across all needles prior to knitting the second half (in the main colour). Reset the needles as follows:

1. 20 needles in HP, 8 needles in WP, 20 needles in HP.
2. Move the carriage across to the part where the last needle in HP and the 1st needle in WP is under the yarn-feed.
3. Thread up with yarns and knit as above with the main difference being that the needles pushed into WP are all left in the same position. Steps 4–7 refer to all makes of machine.
4. When all the needles are back in WP, knit 2 rows of black.
5. Pick up the loops of the original 2 rows of black (knitted prior to the partial-knit section) and place them on adjacent needles which contain loops from the last row of knitting.
6. Knit both loops off together, and cast off.
7. Knit 2 rows of gold in plain-knit.

CHAPTER 6
Slitted Surfaces and Mixed Techniques

It is relatively easy to make a vertically slitted, multi-coloured surface using plain knit, holding position and a mixture of yarns varying in colour or texture. To achieve a more complex type of surface, various combinations of techniques can be employed. For example, two-colour patterned knit can be combined with holding position (fig 148); a mixture of plain and patterned surfaces can be mixed with holding position to produce either slits or patterns (fig 149); intarsia knit technique can be modified so that particular sections of knit are not linked, and horizontal slits can be created using drawn-thread or cast-off methods.

As you delve into the possibilities and explore these combinations of techniques, you will realize that the slits in the knitting give unlimited potential for experimental layered collections of knitted fabrics. These might include woven and printed fabric linings, as well as knitted underlays (see fig 150).

As a general note of advice, I would suggest that

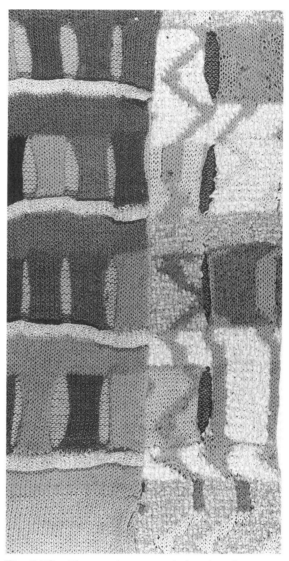

Fig 149. *Plain and patterned slitted surfaces in cottons, wool and chenille (partial knit method).*

Fig 148. *Patterned and slitted surface combining wools, rayon, chenille and lurex (partial knit method).*

Fig 150. *Detail of knitted jacket. Horizontal slits using the drawn thread method.*

Fig 151. *Slitted surface, varying the size of individual sections.*

---

you plan well in advance, firstly in sketch-books and then on graph-paper. This will allow you to visualize the finished piece as well as providing a means of checking numbers of rows and stitches for any given section.

Personally I find it easier to work purely from a graph which utilizes some written instructions. The written versions are merely an aid to an understanding of a particular method of working showing how each section links together.

It is a good idea to look for suitable design source material that will relate to the techniques being used, for example buildings, scaffolding, architectural features, townscapes, factory buildings and skyscraper blocks.

A number of samples follow which show basic methods of working. Each one can be developed in any number of ways to suit your individual needs.

Slitted surfaces samples

Sample 1 (fig 152) – The basic technique
This sample demonstrates the basic techniques used to produce vertically slitted, plain-knit fabric. It can be made on any machine with a partial knit facility. A slitted surface produced in this way, with an underlay of plain knit is shown in fig 151. I suggest using the following colours for a similar sample:

Cream (A)
Light grey (B)
Dark grey (C)

Use a suitable tension and cast on 40 stitches using the wind-on method. Carriage on the right. Knit 1 row.

Work the sample section by section in numerical order, (yarn colours noted as A, B or C).

Section 1 (Band 1):
With the carriage at the left-hand side, knit 10 rows plain knit in Colour A.

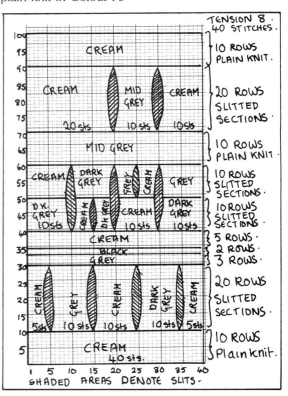

Fig 152. *Sample 1. Pattern diagram.*

Section 2 (Band 2, fig 152):
Set the carriage to HP. Push 30 needles at the right-hand side into hold. Work on the needles left in WP for section 2.

Starting with the carriage on the left, knit 20 rows in Colour A.

It is advisable at this point to remove the cast-on comb (if used) and to weight each section to be knitted either by hand, or using the claw-weights.

Section 3 (Band 2, fig 152):
Push the needles worked on for section 2 into HP. Push 10 needles for section 3 into WP using a multi-eyed transfer-tool.

Knit 20 rows of plain knit on the selected needles in Colour B.

Note:
Before commencing to knit section 3, hang claw-weights directly under the area to be knitted, but not too close to the carriage. Move the carriage slowly over section 2 without the yarn threaded up but with the yarn-feed open. As soon as the needles in WP are visible, stop the carriage just prior to the first needle in section 3 and thread up. Hold the yarn-end whilst the first row is being knitted.

Section 4 (Band 2, fig 152):
Starting with the carriage on the left, follow the procedure for Section 3 using Colour A over 20 rows. Cancel HP. Continue in this manner until all 20 row sections in this band have been knitted.

Section 5 (Band 3, fig 152):
With carriage on the left and using Colour B, knit 10 rows across all 40 needles.
Reset carriage for HP.

Section 6 (Band 4, fig 152):
With carriage on the left continue knitting with Colour B. First push 30 needles on the right into HP. Knit 10 rows over 10 stitches.
Change to Colour C. Knit 10 rows.
Push needles for section 7 into HP.

Section 7–10 (Band 4, fig 152):
Using the transfer-tool push down the next 5 needles into WP.

Using the method of section 2 onwards knit 10 rows in Colour A. Push these 5 needles into HP.

Knit the following 5 needles in colour C, then knit the 10 stitch section directly above these two sections.

Push these needles into HP. Push down the next 10 needles into WP. Knit 10 rows in colour A.

Section 11:
Push 5 needles into HP on the right of section 11 (ready for section 13).

Continue knitting with Colour C on the 5 needles in WP on the left for 10 rows. Push these needles into HP.

Section 12:
Push the next 5 needles into WP.
Knit 10 rows in Colour A. Push the needles back to HP.

Section 13:
Push down the remaining 10 needles into WP.
Knit 10 rows in Colour C.

Section 14:
Continue knitting on these needles for 10 more rows using Colour B.

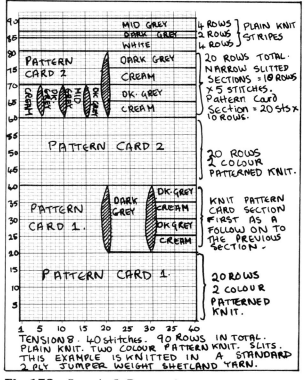

Fig 153. *Sample 2. Pattern diagram.*

Section 15 (Band 5):
Cancel HP on the carriage.
Knit 10 rows in Colour B.
Reset the carriage for HP.

At this point the method of knitting does not vary from that used in Sections 1–15. The number of needles used and the number of rows involved are shown in fig 152:

Section 21:
Cancel HP.
Knit 10 rows in Colour A in plain knitting and cast off.

Sample (fig 153 and 154) – a variation
This sample shows how to work vertical slitted surfaces using plain and patterned areas with holding position. It has twelve sections. Only four basic colours are shown but you can use more if you wish. However, it is better to stick to a small range of colours until you get the hang of the technique. Set your own tension to suit your yarn, I used tension 9:

Cream Shetland (A)
Light grey Shetland (B)
Dark grey Shetland (C)
White Shetland (D)

The areas of patterned knit make use of the patterns in Chapter 3 *i.e.* those based on black-and-white half-timbered buildings. The strong horizontal and vertical elements in the pattern lend themselves well to this type of mixed technique, enabling the knitter to work sections differing in scale and type.

As most of the details of technique are written out in full for Sample 1, I have not repeated details of technique which are given there. If new methods are introduced, they will be dealt with as they arise. Refer constantly to the graph in fig 153 for layout, numbers of rows and stitches, and order of pattern blocks.

Section 1:
Cast on 40 stitches.
Knit 20 rows of Section 1 in Colours C and D using a pattern card.
Place carriage at the right and set for HP.
Do not break off the yarn.

Section 2 (Band 2):
Push 20 needles on the left to HP.
Continue knitting in pattern as for Section 1, on the 20 needles now left in WP.
Break off the yarns and push these needles into HP.

Section 3 (Band 2):
10 needles in WP.
Carriage set for plain knit.
Using Colour B knit 20 rows.
Push needles back to HP.

Section 4 (Band 2):
10 needles in WP on left-hand edge.
Knit 5 rows in Colour A.
Knit 5 rows in Colour C.
Knit 5 rows in Colour A.
Knit 5 rows in Colour C.

Fig 154. *Sample 2. Close-up section.*

Section 5 (Band 3):
Return all needles to WP.
Set needles without knitting any rows.
Using Pattern Card B, from the collection in Chapter 1, Colour A (yarn-feed 1) and Colour B (feed 2), knit 20 rows.
Reset for HP.

Section 6 (Band 4):
With the carriage at left-hand side, knit 10 stitches and 10 rows in Colour A.

Sections 7, 8 and 9 are as Section 6, but using Colours C, B and C respectively.

Section 10:
Working on right-hand 20 needles, knit 5 rows in Colours A, B, C, and D respectively (total 20 rows).

Section 11:
Carriage on the left.
It is now necessary to set the needles for a pattern row without actually knitting. How you do this depends on your make of machine – check the instruction manual for details.
Having set the needles:
Knit 10 rows of 2-colour pattern knit in Colours A (feed 1) and B (feed 2) on the pre-set needles.

Section 12 (Band 5):
Reset the carriage for plain knit.
Knit 4 rows in Colour D.
Knit 2 rows in Colour C.
Knit 4 rows in Colour B.
Cast off.

Sample 3 (fig 155) – more complex slit shapes
This sample combines plain and patterned slitted sections, both rectangular and triangular in form. It introduces the use of triangular-shaped wedges of pattern made from a combination of plain and patterned knitting, using HP. The method is described in detail in Chapter 8. I have used the pattern-cards designed previously, as in the last sample.

By now you should be feeling more confident about working directly from graphs and diagrams (which of necessity contain a minimum of written information) and exploring the many creative applications of each particular method.

A graph or diagram can become a basic framework from which a series of experiments or exercises can be derived. You should try altering the colours, the tension and the type of pattern used. In this way you

Fig 155. *Sample 3. Close-up section. Triangular sections bottom left.*

Fig 156. *Examples of more complex patterned and triangular shapes, see Chapter 8 for method.*

will develop your own creative abilities while the technical details should become second nature.

Section 1
Cast on 40 stitches. Knit 20 rows using Pattern Card B from the previously designed collection (Chapter 1). White yarn, feed 1; Dark Grey yarn, feed 2.

Section 2
Carriage on the left, set for HP. Position of yarns remains unchanged. Push 20 needles on the right into HP and work triangle A using Pattern Card B. Push 1 needle out into HP on each row, at the opposite end to the carriage in order to knit the triangles. Work triangle B in the same manner using Pattern Card F, and Mid-grey yarn in feed I, Dark grey yarn in feed 2. Work infill triangles separately in plain knit stripes using the same method to create the triangles, *i.e.* four rows each of Cream, Dark grey, White, Dark grey and Cream respectively.

Section 3
Use Pattern Card B. Preset needles without actually knitting a row (see individual manuals). Knit 10 rows with Cream yarn in feed 1, Dark grey in feed 2.

Section 4
Continue using Pattern Card B with the positions of the yarns unchanged from the previous section. Push 25 needles into HP on the RHS. Commence knitting on the LHS over the remaining 15 needles still in WP. Knit 20 rows. Push these 15 needles into NWP. Now work over the remaining 25 needles in groups of 50.

Sections 5, 6, 7, 8 and 9
Each section is 10 rows long, and is worked over 5 stitches in plain-knit using Mid grey, White, Mid grey, Cream and Mid grey yarns.

Section 10
Working over the complete 25 stitches from Sections 5, 6, 7, 8 and 9, knit 3 rows in Dark grey, 3 rows in White, and 4 rows in Dark grey. Push all 40 needles back into WP.

Section 11
Using Pattern Card A from the previously designed collection (Chapter 1) preset the needles and knit 20 rows. DK Grey yarn feed 1 and Cream yarn in feed 2.

Section 12
Push 30 needles into HP on the LHS, carriage on the right. Knit 20 rows using Pattern Card No1; Light grey yarn in feed 1, White yarn in feed 2. Push these 10 needles into NWP. Now work over the remaining 30 needles in groups of 10. The same 30 needles are used for the following sections 16, 17, 18 and 19, in different groupings.

Sections 13, 14 and 15
Each section is 10 stitches wide and 10 rows deep. Continue to use Pattern Card A.
Section 13: Feed 1, Light grey; Feed 2, DK Grey.
Section 14: Feed 1, Light grey; Feed 2, Cream.
Section 15: Feed 1, Light grey; Feed 2, White.

Sections 16, 17, 18, 19
Each section is knitted in plain knit, commencing from the left.
Section 16: 5 stitches × 10 rows in Cream.
Section 17: 10 stitches × 10 rows in Dark grey.
Section 18: 10 stitches × 10 rows in Cream.
Section 19: 5 stitches × 10 rows in Dark grey.

Section 20
Using Pattern Card A knit 5 rows with the card on lock, and 5 rows with the card on normal rotation; use Dark grey and White yarns. Knit 2 rows Plain knit. Cast off.

Fig 157. *Horizontal slits – cast-off method.*

Fig 158. *Horizontal slits – drawn thread method.*

Sample 4 (fig 157) – horizontal slits or gaps
Although HP can be used if you want vertical gaps, horizontal gaps require different methods. Use either the cast-on-and-off method or the 'drawn thread' option. This sample involves casting on and casting off to forms the slits, as for a buttonhole.
Cast on 20 stitches with cream wool, tension 9.
Knit 10 rows.
Working over the centre 10 stitches, cast these off using a separate end of wool.
Now cast on (wind-on) over the same 10 stitches.
In order to avoid an untidy gap, manually knit off one stitch to the right of the cast on/off, and one to the left, during the operation.
Knit 10 rows in cream wool.

Sample 5 (fig 158) – horizontal slits; drawn thread version
This example demonstrates the drawn thread method of producing horizontal slits. I do *not*

recommend this method with two-colour pattern knit, as the floats get confused with the line of stitches to be picked up. Sample 4 really is more successful with this type of knitting.

1. Use a suitable tension. Cast on 40 stitches.
2. Knit 10 rows.
3. Using a completely separate end of yarn (preferably cotton or a similar smooth, strong yarn) manually knit off the centre 20 stitches, leaving ends of thread hanging at both right- and left-hand sides.
4. Repeat the last two steps three more times.
5. Knit 10 rows and cast off.
6. Working on Section A and with the reverse side of the knitting facing, pick up the row of 20 stitches directly under the cotton thread.
7. Knit 1 row across these stitches, using dark grey wool, and cast off.
8. Now pick up onto the needles the line of 20 stitches directly above the cotton thread.
9. Knit 1 row in dark grey (it is easier to knit these stitches off if the needles are pushed to FP).
10. Cast off, then draw out the cotton thread.
11. You should now be left with a gap bound on both edges by cast off rows in grey wool.
12. Repeat this method. Vary the number of rows knitted prior to casting off.
13. When the slits are all complete, pick up the complete piece of knitting (with the smooth side facing) and knit in two-colour pattern for the lining.
14. Cast off and link the two pieces together.

Obviously the slit could be varied in width, and also where it is situated. The background lining could be any number of suitable patterns. Try experimenting with several variations of composition and backgrounds.

Fig 159 shows a group of samples demonstrating various ideas for hems, backgrounds and the actual slitted surface. I used these samples as a basis for designing the jacket shown in fig 150.

Fig 159. *Group of samples developing ideas for panels in jackets or coats, using slitted surfaces against various backgrounds and hems.*

CHAPTER 7
Shapes applied on to knitted backgrounds

This chapter should appeal to knitters who enjoy working with geometric structures and patterned surfaces. The main emphasis is on an interesting use of yarns, and strong simple shapes in varying proportions, colour and tonal combination.

You may find that if you do not like working pictorially, then this technique could well be for you. Ideas can be plotted quite simply on to graph-paper using pencil or felt-tip pen.

Combining knitted backgrounds with applied vertical stripes

The first set of samples in this Chapter looks at how to set narrow, vertical strips of knitting against a pre-

viously knitted backing-piece, which I will refer to as the base. In this set of examples, the strips will be applied to the purl face of the base. The knit face can be used, but is slightly more difficult and requires a little experience to deal with. Basically, the strips are knitted on to the base one by one in the following manner.

Take the already knitted base, which in this case comprises horizontal stripes knitted in alternate colours beginning and ending with several rows of waste yarn. Decide where you want to place the strip. Let us assume that you have decided you want to make a strip 10 stitches wide.

Go to the top of the base, to where the waste-yarn

Fig 160. *Detail of strip coat using a Shetland wool base with rayon and wool strips.*

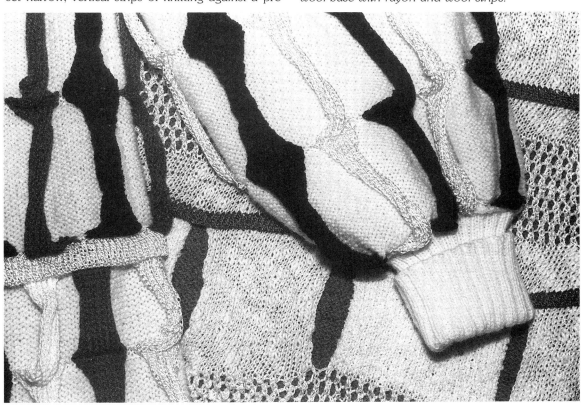

stitches link with the proper stitches, and pick up on to 10 needles a group of 10 stitches at the point you want to put the strip. Make sure that all the other needles are in NWP, and that you haven't picked up waste-yarn stitches in error (this is easily done).

You can now start knitting a strip 10 stitches wide in the chosen colour.

When you have knitted a certain number of rows, stop, park the carriage to one side (leaving the yarn in it) and pick up 10 stitches from the *first* row of the *second* horizontal stripe of the base. These should be the stitches which correspond vertically with the first 10 stitches you picked up to start the process, if you want the strip to proceed vertically down the finished piece. Completion of this step should leave two stitches on each of the 10 needles.

Knit some more of the strip, then do the same attachment procedure at the next junction of horizontal stripes. Proceed in this way, attaching the strip at each junction of stripes, until you reach the bottom waste-yarn junction. Pick up 10 stitches here (*not* the waste-yarn), knit a single row, and cast off, using the strip yarn for this.

The idea is to place these vertical strips across the full width of the base. Once this is done, the waste-yarn can be removed top and bottom without fear of runs.

Obviously you need to take care when you come to remove the waste yarn that all stitches are accounted for. It is best to work systematically from one side (say the left) of the base to the other. If you want strips of constant width, divide the total number of stitches in the base by the number of strips you intend to use – so that a base of, say, 90 stitches width could have 9 strips each 10 stitches wide (or 10 strips 9 stitches wide!).

This basic method can be varied to produce triangles and other assorted shapes, by simply increasing and/or decreasing as you knit the strips.

It doesn't matter if you only have a couple of stitches to pick up at the stripe-junctions on the base – it isn't structurally necessary to pick up here at all if the design you have in mind doesn't need it. However, the stitches at the top and bottom of the base must be accounted for somehow, either by attachment to the strips or by some other method such as binding off or overlocking, or runs will occur (see fig 161).

Left **Fig 161.** *Triangle cardigan. Plain knit base of wool. The triangles are assorted yarns, including chenille, cotton, wool and lurex. Knitweave is used in the yoke.*

Each of the following samples is cast on in the open-ended method, and 8 rows in waste-yarn are knitted before starting on the main sample piece. A further 8 rows of waste-yarn is knitted at the end of the sample, which is then stripped off the machine in readiness for the additional shapes to be knitted onto it.

Many of the illustrated samples were knitted on a chunky-gauge machine, but they can be knitted on any machine provided that appropriate yarns are knitted at a suitable tension.

Sample 1 (fig 162) – applied strips
Cast on 40 stitches at a suitable tension.
For the background (base) knit three bands of stripes, each 20 rows deep in light colours closely matched in tone.
Colour A has a matt finish, Colour B has a silky sheen.
For the strips, make each one 10 stitches wide by 20 rows per section (a section is the length of strip knitted

Fig 162. *Sample 1. Applied strips.*

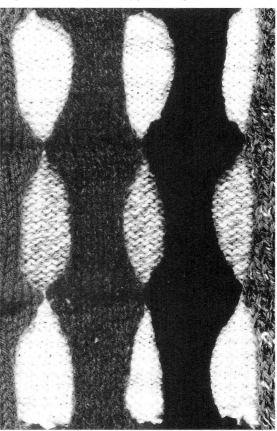

between one row of picked-up base stitches and the next). Use darkish colours in contrasting yarn-types, for example a plain smooth wool, a flecked or slubby yarn.

Sample 2 (fig 163) – applied strips in contrasting widths
Cast on 40 stitches. I used Tension 10.
Background: three bands of stripes each 20 rows deep. Use smooth woollen yarns in dark colours. The colours should have little tonal contrast.
The strips – five in total – are worked as follows:

1. 10 stitches wide
2. 5 stitches wide
3. 10 stitches wide
4. 5 stitches wide
5. 10 stitches wide

Use two contrasting colours and yarns for the strips. For Colour A I used Beige 100% mercerised cotton from Twilleys (Stalite), while B is a tweed-type wool in Dark Mauve from Hayfield. Each section of strip is 20 rows deep to match the background or base.

Sample 3 (fig 164) – stepped pick up points
Cast on 40 stitches. I used Tension 10.
Background: six bands of stripes, each 10 rows deep

Fig 164. *Sample 3. Applied strips*

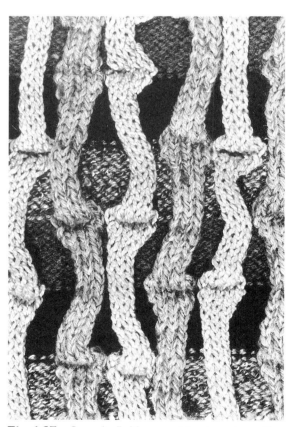

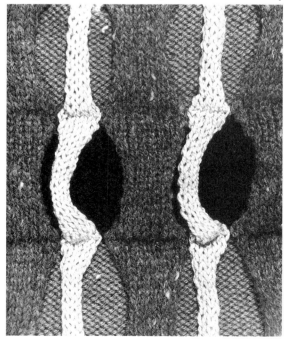

Fig 163. *Sample 2. Applied strips in two contrasting widths.*

Fig 165. *Sample 5. Narrow strips in pairs, with various pick-up points.*

in Beige cotton, alternating with Dark Blue cotton (Twilleys).

Strips: four, each 10 stitches wide. Alternate strips are knitted into the base at different points:

On strips A and C the pick-up points are 1, 3, 5 and 7. On strips B and D pick up at points 2, 4, 6 and 7. If you have difficulty in gauging where on the backing the strips should be attached, mark the backing before you start knitting the strips by threading short pieces of thread through the appropriate stitches. You can do this while you are actually knitting the striped backing.

Sample 4

This is a development of the previous sample. Try combining stepped pick-up points for the strips where the strips are alternately narrow and wide.

Cast on 40 stitches. Use a suitable tension.
Background: six bands of stripes, each 10 rows deep, alternating Colour A (Beige) and Colour B (Cream).
Strips: divide each strip into two of 5 stitches each. The pick-up points are as in the last sample.

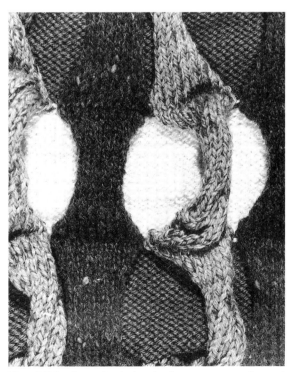

Fig 166. *Sample 6. Applied strips – straight and twisted.*

Sample 5 (fig 165) – using narrower strips

Cast on 40 stitches. Use a suitable tension.
Background: bands of stripes, each 10 rows deep, using Colours A, B and C.
Strips: all are five stitches wide, and are hooked up into the background in pairs at alternate junctions between stripes.

Sample 6 (fig 166) – combining twisted and straight strips

Cast on 40 stitches. Use a suitable tension.
Background: bands of stripes each 20 rows deep, alternating light and dark colours.
Strips: each 10 stitches wide. Strips A and C are 20 rows per section, while B and D are 30 rows per section and are twisted once before being attached to the backing.

Sample 7 (fig 167, right) – using more than one colour

Cast on 40 stitches and work 60 rows at a suitable tension in the following ways:
Backing: using a light and dark colour knit alternating stripes in bands of 20 rows each;
Strips: 10 stitches wide, 20 rows deep per section. Each strip is knitted thus;
15 rows in Colour A and 5 rows in Colour B. Pick-up on the base and repeat to complete the full length of the strip. Colour A changes on each consecutive strip, while Colour B remains the same.

Sample 8 (fig 167, left) – combining variations of colours and widths

Cast on 40 stitches and work 60 rows at a suitable tension in the following ways:
Background: this is the same as the previous sample.
Strips: these alternate in widths of 10 stitches and 5 stitches. The 10-stitch strip is knitted using 15 rows of Colour A and 5 rows of Colour B as before. The strip of width 5 stitches is always Colour B.

Many variations of this technique are possible. For example you could attach beads or sequins at the linking points, or the strips could be pulled together and stitched down at certain points to form a honeycomb pattern. Again beads or sequins could be added as a decorative feature at these points.

Fig 167. *Sample 7 (right). Applied strips.*
Sample 8 (left). Applied strips.

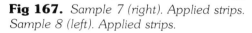

Applying triangles and asymmetrical shapes to plain or patterned bases

The samples in this section develop the type of unit which can be applied to a plain or patterned knitted base. The method is essentially the same as for those samples in Group 1, the main difference being the shape and positioning of the overlays.

The purl face of the base and the knit face of the applied shape are used in all the samples.

Sample 9 (fig 169, right) – triangles
This sample was knitted on a chunky gauge machine at Tension 10 over 20 stitches. If you are using another machine type, adjust the tension to suit. Two contrasting colours (A and B) are used for the base.

Knit several rows of waste yarn.
Knit 4 stripes, each of 10 rows, alternating the 2 colours (40 rows in total).
Remove from the machine using waste yarn.
Using the same principle as the overlaid strips, work from the right hand side of the knitting with the purl side faces the knitter. Replace the first 10 stitches of the first row of knitting (*not* waste yarn) back on to the needles in WP.
Do not remove the waste yarn at this stage – it is holding the remaining 10 stitches which have still to be worked on.

Fig 168. *Applied triangles decorated with beads.*

136

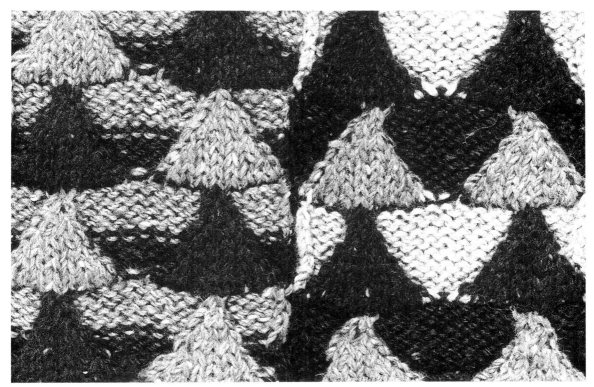

Fig 169. *Samples 9 (right) and 10 (left).*
Knit-facing plain triangles on a purl-facing base.

Knit in Colour C across all ten needles in WP. On the next and every following 7 rows, decrease 1 stitch at the beginning of each row (use the double-eyed transfer tool).

Two stitches now remain on the machine.

Break off Colour C yarn.

Push forward to WP 4 needles either side of, and including, the remaining 2 stitches (10 needles in all). Thread up Colour B.

Pick up the first 10 stitches on the right of the *first* row of the *second* band of knitting on the backing (exactly as you did for strips).

Make another triangle in Colour A. To make it easier to knit the first row of the triangle, push out all 10 needles to a forward position so that the stitches fall behind the needle latches. Note that there will be double stitches on the two central needles.

Repeat the process until your sample is covered with small knitted triangles.

To complete the sample, remove the waste yarn at top and bottom.

Sample 10 (fig 169, left) – a variation
Knit the background in stripes, each of 5 rows and alternating in Colours A and B. Each triangle will still cover a height of 10 rows, but will span two stripes on the base or backing. Use colours which are closely related to achieve a subtler effect than Sample 9, so emphasising the reverse areas of purl against the plain knit.

Sample 11 (fig 170) – using contrasting colours
The backing is knitted in sequences of 10 rows, alternating two relatively close colours. The applied shapes contrast strongly, being much lighter and brighter. Compare the results with the previous sample.

The overlay shape is worked over 10 rows. One edge is completely straight, the other is slanted. To make the slant, a decrease is effected *on the same side* before each of the 10 rows is knitted (total of 10 decreases). This will produce a right-angled triangle.

A variation of this sample could be made by either altering the height of the backing stripes, and consequently the overlaid shapes, or simply varying the colour or yarn-type.

A length of mock-tubing completes this sample. To knit a tube in this manner, set the knit-carriage to slip

Fig 170. *Sample 11. Applied shapes.*

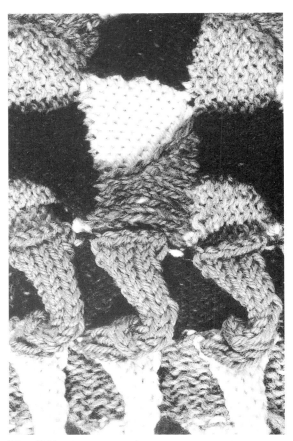

Fig 171. *Examples of asymmetrically shaped triangles with a hem of twisted strips.*

in one direction and knit in the other. A float of yarn will stretch across the knitting in one direction, and when the knitting is removed from the machine, this helps to pull in the knitting to give the appearance of a tube.

Apply the tube either by hand or by machine sewing, depending upon the effect required.

Sample 12 (fig 171) – combining strips and triangles
The base consists of four sections each of 10 rows. All decreasing in the overlay sections takes place on the same side, as follows:

Knit one row without decreasing, then decrease by 1 stitch on each of the following 5 rows. There should remain 3 stitches. Knit 3 rows without shaping.

Pick up 10 stitches from the backing at the next stripe-junction, reversing only the edge where the decreases take place on alternate units.

This sample is completed with a hem comprising light and dark twisted strips.

Intarsia backings with overlays

It is possible to use the intarsia technique in conjunction with applied shapes. A backing can be produced in broken stripes, for example, or a chequerboard unit repeated in a variety of colours or textures.

Sample 13 (fig 173, right) – combining intarsia and triangles
Cast on 20 stitches at Tension 10 (or to suit) using a plain colour. Knit 6 rows in stocking stitch followed by 40 rows of broken stripes using mixed colours. Each stripe is made up of one end of yarn which contains several thin strands of varying texture. The background is completed by knitting another 6 rows of plain knit, then cast off.

To make the triangular overlays, work as for the previous samples (10 stitches by 10 rows). Knit one vertical column of triangles. Leave the next stripe free of triangles.

Originally I had intended to cover the entire base, but halfway through the sample I decided that I liked the contrast between the purl-faced intarsia stripes and the triangular overlays.

Sample 14 (fig 173, left) – a variation
Cast on 20 stitches and work 40 rows as follows:

An intarsia base, made up of rectangles, is knitted (each rectangle 10 rows by 10 stitches). Every alternate rectangle contains an integral triangle knitted into it by the intarsia method. The remaining rectangles are decorated with an applied triangle of 10 rows by 10 stitches.

Sample 15 (fig 174) – intarsia triangle on plain knit
Cast on 20 stitches. Use a suitable tension.
This sample is constructed from a plain knit, striped

Below **Fig 173.** *Samples 13 (right) and 14 (left). Intarsia base with plain-knit triangles.*

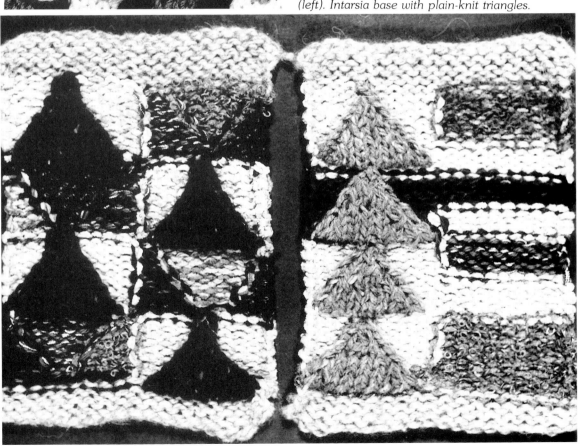

base (10 rows per stripe – 40 rows total). The large overlaid triangle is in intarsia.

The large triangle consists of 20 rows of intarsia knitting decreasing 1 stitch at the beginning of rows 002–018. Two stitches will remain.

To perform the decreases in intarsia, push back into WP the first 3 needles next to the carriage, using a 3-eyed transfer tool. Use a two-eyed tool to make a decrease where the doubled stitch is one needle away from the edge. Manually knit off the decrease and return the needles to the intarsia position.

Smaller plain knit triangles flank the main triangle. On my sample a hem was added. To knit this pick up the first row of knitting of the base with the smooth side facing. Using the intarsia method knit 15 rows in vertical stripes. Continue using this method in order to match the tensions correctly, and knit 15 rows in one colour only for the back of the hem.

Hook the first row of the hem onto corresponding needles. There will now be double stitches on each needle. Push the needles (not the stitches) to a forward position. Thread the yarn through the main tension assembly. Knit 1 row to close the hem, and cast off.

If you decide to develop this sample into a garment, work in the following order:

1. Knit the hem by first casting on and knitting several rows in waste yarn. This will avoid a bulky cast off edge at the back of the hem.
2. Continue by knitting the main backing section.
3. Knit the applied shapes in your chosen style.

This routine could apply to any number of different designs. However check in which direction you require the knit or purl sides of the knitting to face. Remember that you can use waste yarn or the garter-bar to turn the work.

Fig 174. *Sample 15. Intarsia triangles applied to a plain-knit (but purl-facing) base.*

Fig 175. *Sample idea for cardigan with horizontally pleated hem.*

Combining triangles, pattern card and twisted strips on knitted bases

All the main technical problems should now have been dealt with except the use of the pattern card. This can be used most successfully on the overlays rather than the bases following any of the methods already discussed. It is not a suitable technique for the base knitting as it is practically impossible to see the stitches (because of the floats) as junction rows for pick-up points. It is, however, very effective on strips (see photo of coat, fig 1).

You should now try combining various elements to produce larger surfaces in different weights, colours and yarns. Ribbing and hems can be added as in some of my samples, in order to suggest possible ideas for garments.

_____

Fig 176. *Triangle section and hem knitted sideways. A sample idea for a sleeve.*

Do not be afraid to try out new ideas. Sometimes an idea that might seem slightly silly or offbeat can be a sound basis for a successful run of new samples. Try mixing contrasting shapes and colours, such as a vertically pleated hem attached to a main section covered in applied triangles.

A basic pleated hem can be made as follows:
Cast on using waste yarn.
Knit several rows. Change to Colour A.
(*)Knit 10 rows in Colour A.
Change to Colour B. Knit 10 rows. Pick up stitches from the first row in Colour B on to corresponding needles.
Knit 1 row to link the pleat.
Go back to (*) and repeat these steps as many times as required.
Cast off.
Link the hem to the main section one edge at a time.

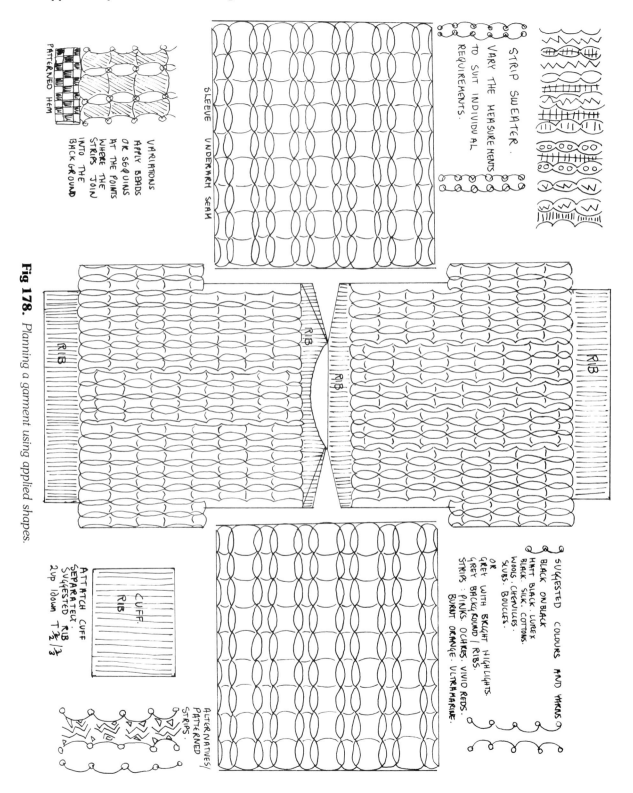

Fig 178. *Planning a garment using applied shapes.*

STRIP SWEATER.

VARY THE MEASUREMENTS
TO SUIT INDIVIDUAL
REQUIREMENTS.

SLEEVE UNDERARM SEAM

PATTERNED HEM

VARIATIONS
APPLY BEADS
OR SEQUINS
AT THE POINTS
WHERE THE
STRIPS JOIN
INTO THE
BACKGROUND

RIB

RIB

RIB

RIB

CUFF.
RIB

ATTACH CUFF
SEPARATELY.
SUGGESTED RIB
2up 100mm T ½/3

ALTERNATIVE/
PATTERNED
STRIPS.

SUGGESTED COLOURS AND YARNS

BLACK ON BLACK
MATT BLACK, LUREX,
BLACK, SILK, COTTONS,
WOOLS, CHENILLES,
SLUBS, BOUCLÉS.

OR
GREY WITH BRIGHT HIGHLIGHTS.
GREY BACKGROUND / RIBS.
STRIPS : PINKS, OCHRES, VIVID REDS,
BURNT ORANGE, ULTRAMARINE.

142

Left **Fig 177.** *Applied triangles divided by bands of pleats, with a standard 2-up, 2-down rib.*

This is just one variation. Several ideas are shown in the photographs suggesting other combinations. Use these as a starting point for your own creations (see figs 175, 176 and 177).

It is relatively easy to create simply constructed garments using this method, but keep the edge shaping to a minimum. A design based on four rectangles could be transformed into a strip sweater, for example, using the following guide. The garments in figs 1, 160 and 161 were based on this idea.

Knit sections A, B, C and D in stocking stitch as a series of stripes, to act as a base for the strips, triangles or whatever you decide to apply.

For these sections you will need to cast on a number of stitches divisible by the number of stitches needed for the strips. For example, 160 stitches

Below **Fig 179.** *Close-up section of the back of an appliqué jacket. Knitweave base with cut-out shapes in knitted lace and knitweave.*

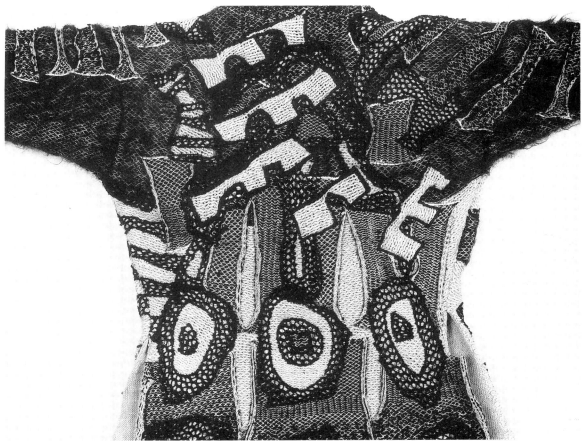

143

Fig 180. *Design idea for a knitted jacket using knitweave, knitted lace, plain knit in combination with quilting and machine embroidery.*

would allow for 16 strips each 10 stitches wide, or 8 strips each 20 stitches, or even 4 at 20 stitches alternating with 8 at 10 stitches (see fig 178).

Each section should be cast on and off in waste yarn. The ribs for all the welts and the neckband can be attached after the main sections have been completely decorated and the ends sewn in.

In order to draw the sleeves in at the cuff, the ribs should be worked on fewer stitches than the main section. For example, if sections D and C are cast on with 120 stitches then the cuff should be about 60 stitches.

A long cuff made to turn back will work success-

fully. I also knit the main welts on fewer stitches than the strip section. For example, if the full width of the sweater requires 160 stitches, a rib of 140 stitches would give good results. Again, make these ribs reasonably long to balance the body section.

The shoulder and neck ribbed section would equal the amount of stitches in the main body – in our example 160 stitches.

A straight slash neckline would be suitable, but alternatively try adding a collar or neckband.

Stitching applied shapes on to a background

Shapes can be knitted to size using various methods of increasing and decreasing, or they can be cut from

144

Fig 181. *Appliqué jacket in wear.*

Fig 182. *Diagram showing ideas for simple motifs for appliqué.*

strips of knitted fabric and applied to a suitable backing such as knitweave, single- or double-bed Jacquard (see figs 179, 180 and 181).

The base can be backed with wadding to give the decorated surface more depth. Remember, however, that the knitting will lose its elasticity. When designing garments using this technique, you must take this fact into account.

On a practical note, before applying a design to a knitted base, tack the wadding and the backing knit into a flat sandwich, two layers deep. This will help to keep the structure stable and stop the wadding moving out of position.

As for other techniques, plan the position of the applied shapes in advance. Either sketch in rough suggestions for where the design should be placed, or pin cut-out paper shapes to the backing until you are satisfied with the arrangement, then replace with the real thing.

Pin, tack, and finally machine-sew into position. If the applied shapes are to be cut from a length of knitting, prior to cutting out, machine a row of close, straight stitching close to the edge to be cut. This should stop the knitting from unravelling. Sew on to the base with a straight stitch on the same line as the first row of stitching, then finish this off by using a close zigzag stitch to cover both raw edges and the original line of stitching.

My examples show a fitted jacket constructed in this way. Many of the pattern pieces were cut from lace knitting and applied over knitweave, creating a patterned and textured surface. The technique can put to use in other ways, for example to create single motifs, or to liven up certain areas of a garment, such as the yoke of a jacket (fig 182).

145

CHAPTER 8
Unusual combinations of technique

This chapter considers ways in which different techniques can be combined to produce unusual surfaces. Intarsia, partial knit, patterning, simple ribs and slitted surfaces are all considered, as is the development of quilted surfaces touched on in the last chapter. It may even be appropriate (particularly if you are good at dressmaking) to combine other fabrics with knit, such as suedette, jersey, and felted fabrics. There are many possibilities to be explored here.

Simple Geometric patterns using shaped intarsia and partial knit

Figs 184 and 185 show the main segments of the first five knitted samples and sample 6 worked up. Although each segment is drawn as a separate shape

---

Fig 183. *Three shaped samples using intarsia, partial knit, and 2-colour patterned knitting.*

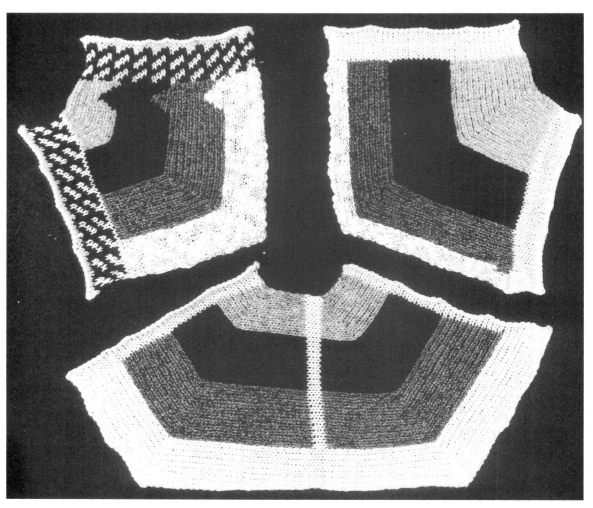

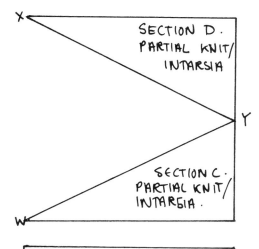

SECTION F. PLAIN KNIT.

SECTION E.
INTARSIA.

X

SECTION D.
PARTIAL KNIT/
INTARSIA

Y

SECTION C.
PARTIAL KNIT/
INTARSIA.

W

SECTION B.
INTARSIA.

SECTION A.
PLAIN KNIT.

NOTE. SECTIONS 'C' and 'D'
ARE LINKED. EDGE WY and YX
FORM SHAPED SECTION.

Fig 184. *Diagram showing shapes of individual segments.*

Fig 185. *Samples 1–6 (right to left) worked in intarsia and partial knitting.*

in the diagram, they are all linked as a continuous piece of knitting.

The yarns used in this section are a wool 4-ply equivalent:

Medium grey (A)
Bright pink (B)
White (C)

Colours B and C are an anti-tickle yarn, superwash quality available from King Kole Yarns (see suppliers).

Wind off small bobbins of Colours B and C for the intarsia sections.

All samples in this group are knitted over 40 stitches.

Sample 1 (fig 186)
Section A: Knit 6 rows in Colour A.
Section B: Set needles for intarsia, and do as follows:
With the intarsia carriage on the right, commence laying in yarns over selected needles, from the right, and in the following order:
30 needles Colour C.

147

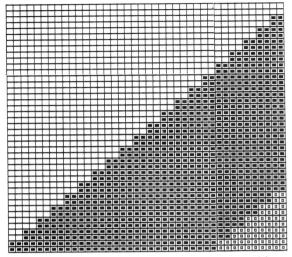

Fig 186. *Sample 1, pattern graph for partial knit section (c).*

10 needles Colour B.

Knit 10 rows in this arrangement.

Carriage on the right.

Section C:

Continue in intarsia:

Set the carriage to Partial Knit.

Push 2 needles on the left into HP. Knit 1 row to the left.

Loop the yarn under the last needle in HP to avoid a hole appearing, before knitting to the right (continue to do this throughout these samples). Knit to the right.

Continue in this manner, putting two more needles into HP every alternate row, until all 40 needles are in HP.

Section D:

Reverse the process of Section C until all the needles are back in WP.

Section E:

As Section B.

Section F:

As Section A.

Sample 2

The intarsia design is varied in segments C and D. In Section C, Colour B advances 2 needles to the right every alternate row until all stitches are in Colour B, while the area knitted in Colour C gradually diminishes (see fig 185).

Continue to knit in Colour B only, until the remainder of the needles are in HP, as in the first example.

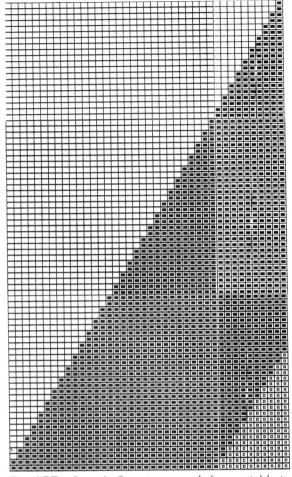

Fig 187. *Sample 3, pattern graph for partial knit section.*

In Section D the process is reversed, putting pairs of needles back into WP and re-introducing Colour C after X rows – refer to the graph in fig 186.

Knit until all needles are back in WP.

Sample 3 (fig 187)

Alterations are made to the main partial knit sections (C and D), by advancing Colour B by 1 stitch only, on every alternate row (see fig 185) and putting one needle into HP on alternate rows.

Sample 4

Knit as in Sample 3, varying the arrangement of the colours. Colours A and B are reversed in Sections B and C. They exchange places again in Sections D and E.

148

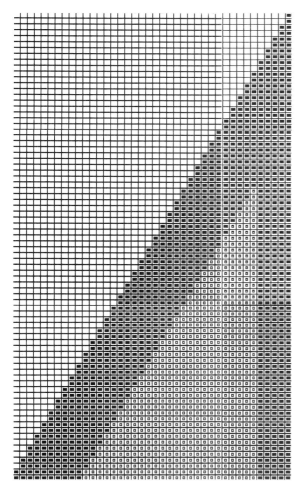

Fig 188. *Sample 4, pattern graph for partial knit section.*

Sample 5 (fig 188)

The intarsia section uses a different needle arrangement. From right to left the arrangement is:

5 needles: colour B.
25 needles: colour C.
10 needles: colour B.

The five needles in Colour B on the right-hand edge remain constant in Colour B. All other instructions are as for Sample 3.

Sample 6 (fig 189)

The shape of the sample is altered (see fig 185). A straight section is introduced (D).

Sections A, B, C, and E, F and G are knitted as in Sample 3.

Section D is knitted in plain knit for 6 rows in Colour B.

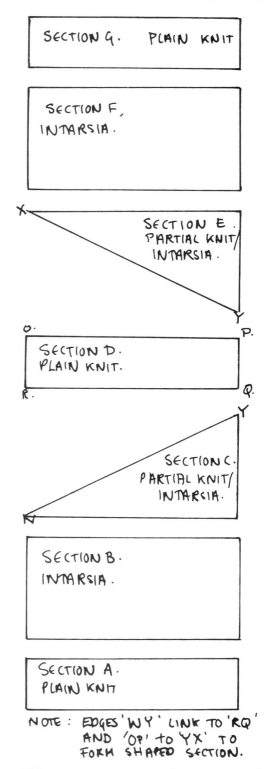

Fig 189. *Sample 6. Diagram showing order of segments.*

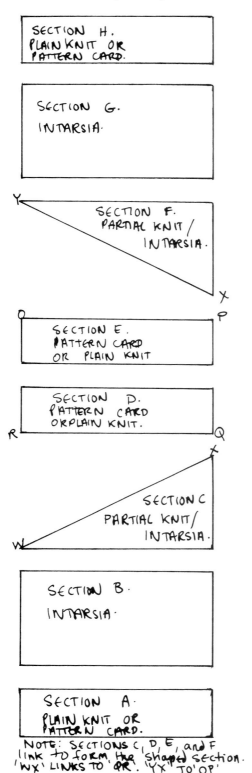

SECTION H.
PLAIN KNIT OR
PATTERN CARD.

SECTION G.
INTARSIA.

SECTION F.
PARTIAL KNIT /
INTARSIA.

SECTION E.
PATTERN CARD
OR PLAIN KNIT

SECTION D.
PATTERN CARD
OR PLAIN KNIT.

SECTION C
PARTIAL KNIT/
INTARSIA.

SECTION B.
INTARSIA.

SECTION A.
PLAIN KNIT OR
PATTERN CARD.

NOTE: SECTIONS C, D, E, and F
link to form the 'shaped section.
'WX' LINKS TO 'QR'. 'YX' TO 'OP'

Fig 190. *Diagram for Sample 7 knitted in eight segments.*

Sample 7

A development of the previous sample with eight main sections (see fig 190).

Sections A, B, C and D substitute Colour A for Colour B, and *vice versa*.

Sections E, F, G and H return the colours to their original positioning.

Section D is knitted plain for 6 rows in Colour C. Section E, 6 rows in Colour B.

As a general principle, these samples demonstrate a useful method for producing, for example, sideways-knitted skirts, collar-type shapes, and yokes. Regard each section of a sample as a single-unit building block, which can then be repeated X number of times. A continuous piece of knitting can be made which will form some kind of curved shape, with wide and narrow edges; fig 192 shows a shaped collar over a slitted dress. Other such units can be introduced at

Fig 191. *Collection of shaped samples 7–11 in plain knit, intarsia and two-colour patterned knit.*

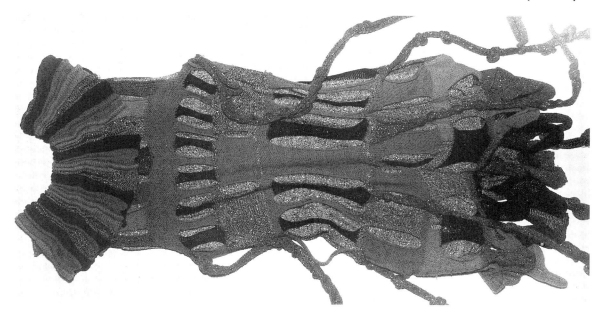

Fig 192. *Pleated shaped collar using partial knitting complementing the dress (slitted surface technique in plain knitting).*

regular intervals to alter the overall shape – see fig 193.

A quick method of trying out ideas for combined shapes follows. Knit up single-unit shape. Measure each shape. Transfer the measurements to a thin sheet of card, and draw an outline. This can be cut out and used as a template to draw around in order to make multiple copies of each shape (brown parcel-paper is suitable for this).

Arrange several units together until you arrive at a suitable shape. Use sticky tape to join them all together. The arrangements may suggest an idea for a detachable collar, for instance.

If you have access to a tailors' dummy, pin the shape on this, making any necessary alterations. For example, would it be better if it were less deep (fewer stitches) or do the triangular units need to be wider (more rows).

When you are satisfied with the outcome, knit a continuous piece. It can very easily be finished into a collar by adding a narrow rib-band on the top edge along with a button-loop fastening (see fig 194).

Quite complex shapes can be achieved if they are worked out section by section. Use a tension square in the appropriate yarns and pattern to approximate rows and stitches. I find trial and error the best method as it is sometimes better to work 'in the

round', adding and subtracting shapes until a solution is arrived at, rather than planning everything meticulously on flat paper.

There is another way of trying out ideas fairly quickly, especially if you own a sewing machine. Purchase a few metres/yards of cheap sweatshirt material or knitted jersey fabric. You can cut shapes from these which, sewn together, simulate a piece of knitting more effectively than paper. I suggest jersey rather than calico for the same reasons.

Combining partial and patterned knit, intarsia and slits

Sample 8
As Sample 7, but knitting alternate stripes in Colours B and C on the 5 right hand edge stitches. A slit is worked over the centre stitches using the drawn thread method.

Change colour every 4 rows.

Sample 9
Refer to Sample 8. Replace Section D (central panel) with a patterned area. The rest of the sample is knitted as before. To knit Section D:
Use the main carriage, and thread up Colours A and B through the main tension assembly.
Knit 1 row in Colour A to set the needles (or pattern drum).
Knit 9 rows in 2-colour pattern. Knit 1 row plain in Colour A. Return all the needles to HP, with the

151

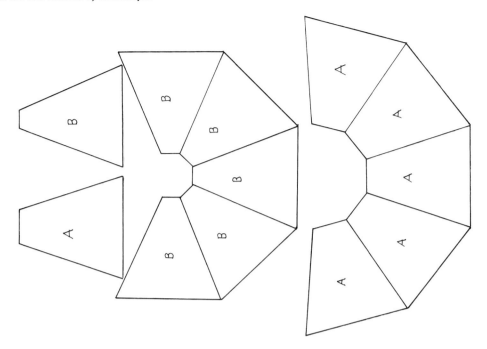

exception of the first 2 needles on the right hand side. Use the transfer tool to push them into the intarsia position.

Continue working in intarsia as in the previous sample.

Sample 10

The central panel is worked by knitting 2 rows in Colour A, followed by 9 rows of 2-colour pattern. The section is completed by knitting 2 more rows in Colour A.

Sample 11

Sections B and C:

Yarn-feed 1, Colour B.
Yarn-feed 2, Colour C.
Rows 000–001, card on lock.
    002–009, normal rotation.

Sections D and E:
Yarn-feeds as previously.
Rows 000–001, card on lock.
    002–005, normal rotation.
    006–009, normal rotation.
    010–011, card on lock.

Fig 193. *Repeating segments of partial knit and straight sections.*

Sample 12 (fig 195)

A composite sample using varying qualities of greys (A), pinks (B) and whites (C). The layout is as the previous sample.

Section A: Knit 6 rows Colour A.

Section B: 2-colour pattern knit – follow chart:

Row Counter	Feed 1	Feed 2	Knit instructions
000–001	B	–	Plain knit, card on lock. Set needles.
001–002	B	C	Card on lock. Patterned knit.
002–010	B	–	Plain knit.

Section C:
Intarsia, as before, but using a variety of textures of yarn.

Sections D and E:
2-colour pattern knit – follow chart:

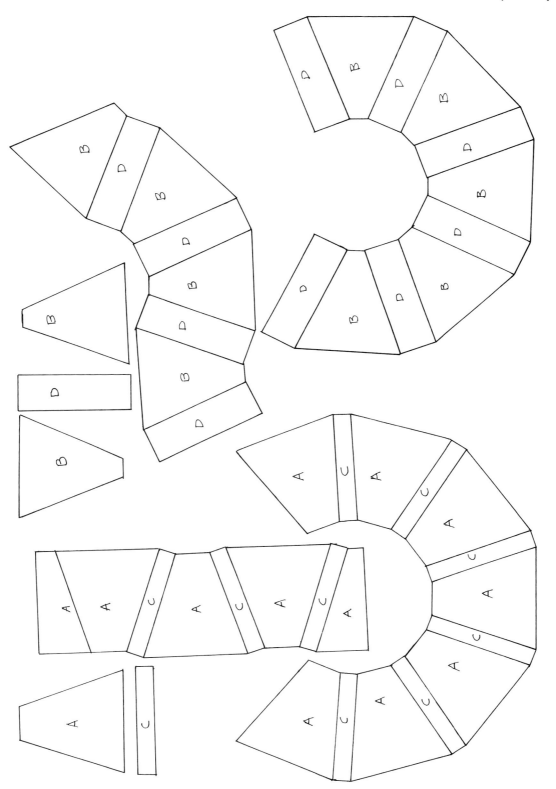

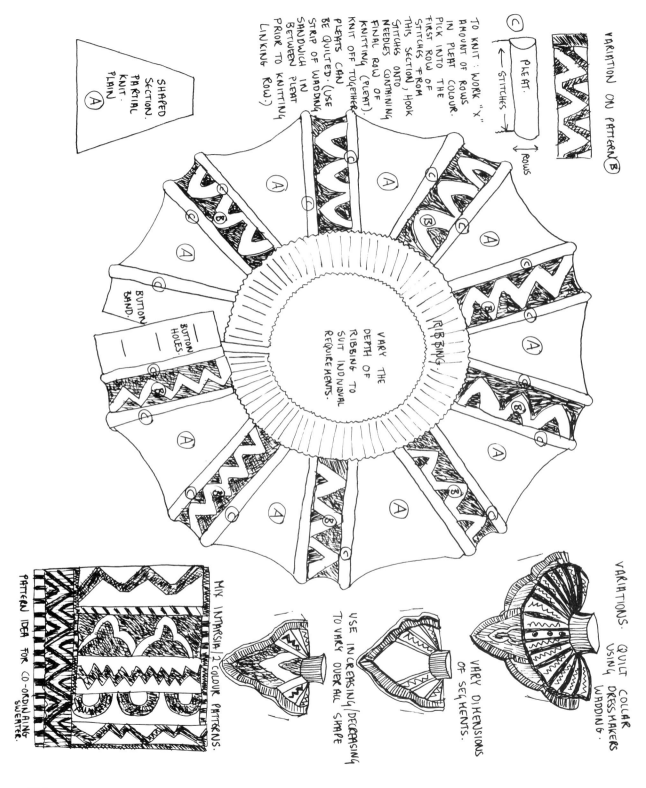

VARIATION ON PATTERN B

SHAPED SECTION. PARTIAL KNIT. PLAIN.

TO KNIT: WORK "X" AMOUNT OF ROWS IN PLEAT COLOUR. PICK INTO THE FIRST ROW OF STITCHES FROM THIS SECTION, HOOK STITCHS ONTO NEEDLES CONTINUING FINAL ROW OF KNITTING (PLEAT). KNIT OFF TOGETHER. PLEATS CAN BE QUILTED. (USE STRIP OF WADDING SANDWICH IN BETWEEN PLEAT PRIOR TO KNITTING LINKING ROW.)

PLEAT — STITCHES — ROWS

VARY THE DEPTH OF RIBBING TO SUIT INDIVIDUAL REQUIREMENTS.

RIBBING.

BUTTON BAND.
BUTTON HOLES.

VARIATIONS. QUILT COLLAR USING DRESS MAKERS WADDING.

VARY DIMENSIONS OF SEGMENTS.

USE INCREASING/DECREASING TO VARY OVERALL SHAPE.

MIX INTARSIA/2 COLOUR PATTERNS.

PATTERN IDEA FOR CO-ORDINATING SWEATER.

154

Fig 195. *Sample 12. Composite using partial knit, patterned knitting and waste-yarn shaping.*

Row Counter	Feed 1	Feed 2	Knit instructions
000–001	B	–	Plain knit, card on lock. Set needles.
001–002	B	C	Card on lock.
002–006	B	C	Card moves.
006–010	C	B	Normal rotation.
010–012	C	B	Card on lock.
012–013	C	–	Plain knit.

Section F:
Reverse of Section C.
Section G:
As Section B.
Repeat from Section B to Section C once more, producing sample with sections A, B, C and D (see fig 195).

To complete this sample, pick up and place on

the machine 60 stitches taken from the narrowest edge of the wedge shape. The purl side of the sample should be facing the knitter. You should find that the rows on the first part of the sample will run horizontally to the knitting machine, whilst the stitches will be at approximate right angles to the needle bed. Use a small pattern and knit 20 rows at Tension 8.

Strip off the machine using waste yarn. Replace the knitting on 50 needles. This means doubling up every fifth needle. (NB: Make sure that you pick up the final row of the patterned knit, and not the first row of waste yarn.)

Knit another 15 rows of pattern. Strip off again with waste yarn. Replace the knitting on 40 needles. Every fourth needle should then contain 2 stitches.

Knit another 10 rows of pattern, followed by 2 rows of plain knitting. Unravel all the waste yarn. The sample should look like the illustration.

The method just described can also be used to shape yokes, sleeves and skirts where the design requires the stitches to run horizontally.

Sample 13
This sample combines intarsia, partial knit and a slitted surface.

155

Fig 196. *Two shaped samples with pleats dividing each section. Samples 14 (right) and 16 (left).*

Section A:
Knit 6 rows in Colour A.
Section B:
Knit 10 rows plain in Colour C.
Section C:
Arrange needles for intarsia thus:
  5 needles Colour C.
25 needles Colour B.
10 needles Colour C.
Work from the graph (fig 188).
Section D:
Knit 6 rows Colour B. Use a separate thread to knit over the centre 20 stitches. This will form the slit. Knit 6 rows. Section E:
As Section C (in reverse).
Section F:
As Section B.
Section G:
As Section A.

This sample could be an idea for a collar, where the main colour of the garment is visible through the slitted area.

A range of more complex samples have also been derived combining these techniques. I have particularly experimented with textured patterns and unusually shaped pieces. The yarns in the samples are mainly supplied by Yeoman Yarns.

Sample 14 (fig 196, right)
Use the following suggested colours:

   Black Opium and Black Grigna (A)
   White Opium and Black and White mix Grigna (B)
   White Cannel Cotton (C)

Section A:
Cast on 40 stitches.
Knit 10 rows in Colour C. Make a pleat in the following manner:
Pick up the first row of stitches using a hook and place onto the equivalent needle on the machine.
This needle will already contain 1 stitch from the last row knitted.
Pick up all 40 stitches.
Holding the knitting down from the carriage, push the needles (but not the stitches) forward, and knit 1 row over all the needles. A linked pleat will result.
Section B:
Carriage on the left. Use a small pattern repeat.
Thread up Colour A and Colour B, and knit in 2-colour pattern putting 2 stitches into HP on the right

on every alternate row until all needles are in HP. The pattern is locked 'elongated' knitted normally in a random sequence. Carriage on the left to finish.
Section C:
Knit 10 rows of Plain knit in Colour C.
Make a pleat as in Section A.
Section D:
As Section B, but reverse left for right throughout. Carriage on the right to finish.
Section E:
As Section C.

Repeat Sections B, C, D and E as many times as required.

Sample 15
Cast on 40 stitches at Tension 8.
Section A:
Make pleat from 10 rows plain knit, in Colour C.
Section B:
Carriage on the left. Set for Partial Knit and patterned knitting using a combination of White Opium yarn and black and white flecked Grigna in yarn feed A and Black Opium yarn mixed with a solid black Grigna in yarn feed B (all available from Yeoman Yarns) Put 1 stitch in to HP on the right on every alternate row until all needles are in HP.
Section C:
Make pleat in Colour C as in Section A.
Section D:
Carriage on the right. Repeat Section B, reversing all left and right instructions.

Sample 16 (fig 196, left)
As Sample 14, but introduce 10 rows of patterned knitting prior to knitting the Partial Knit sections.
   Divide by pleats of 10 rows.

Sample 17 (fig 197, top)
Refer to Sample 16. This variation requires the partial knit sections to be knitted as stated, but additionally knit 2 rows plain, then push all but 2 needles back into HP. Knit in striped bands of plain knit until all the needles are returned to WP. (4 Rows per stripe.)

Sample 18 (fig 197, bottom)
An idea for an exotic collar derived from sample 17, varying the amount of needles put into HP and the direction of each segment.

Fig 198 demonstrates some of the other possibilities of combining plain and patterned areas within a

Fig 197. *Samples 17 (top) and 18 (bottom).*

Fig 198. *Close-up of dress centre front panel using patterned partial knitting.*

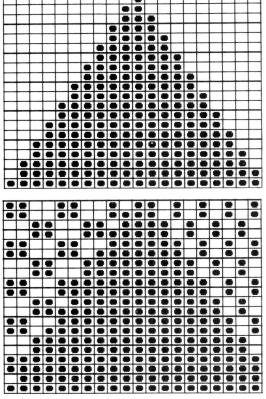

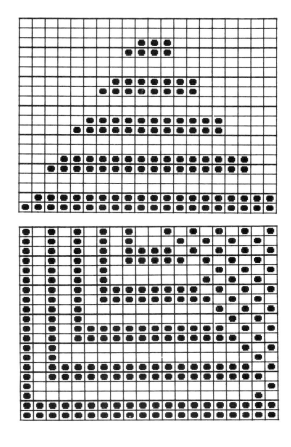

Fig 199. *Pattern graph for triangular sections.*

structured network of triangular and striped surfaces. Fig 156 (page 127) also shows triangles knitted in patterns, plain stripes, and single colours.

The middle sample suggested an idea for a centre back and front panel for the dress featured in fig 198. The frill was constructed using intarsia and partial knit.

Sample 19

This sample shows how to knit plain or patterned triangles and can be developed to suit other shapes and pattern combinations (see figs 198 and 156). Try a sample knitted over 30 stitches.

Knit 10 rows in white wool. Divide the needles as follows:

5 stitches background.
20 stitches panels.
5 stitches background.

Main carriage on the left. Push 5 needles into HP on *both edges*, left and right.

Set the carriage for partial knit. Slowly move the empty carriage across the first 5 needles in HP,

resting it just in front of the first needle in knitting position.

Thread up the dark colour, making certain that it is firmly in the yarn feed. Hold down the loose end. Knit to the right over the centre 20 stitches.

Push 1 needle on the left into HP. Knit to the left. Push 1 needle on the right into HP. Knit to the right. Repeat the last 2 rows ten times in all (20 rows). Carriage on the left. Fill in the left-hand background section thus:

Push the first 5 needles into WP.
Knit 2 rows.
Push 2 more needles into WP on the right.
Knit 2 rows.
Continue pushing pairs of needles into WP on alternate rows ten times in all (20 rows).

Carriage on the right. Work the right-hand side of the background in the same manner.
Cancel HP. Knit 10 rows in White wool.

You should now be armed with enough information to embark on your own experiments. I would suggest keeping clear notes on how the partial knit sections

160

were achieved, particularly regarding the starting point (left or right) of the main carriage for each new section. Try working from the graphs in fig 199 using plain and patterned knit.

Fig 200. *Two-colour zigzag pattern – ribbing and partial knit combined.*

Miscellaneous techniques

Ribbing in conjunction with Partial Knit (figs 200, 201, 202, 203)

I find it easier to knit the shaped ribs at the end of a piece of knitting, or to knit a base of approximately 30 rows straight before going into partial knit.

If you try to knit partial knit ribbing directly after casting on, the cast-on comb will begin to push up between the needle beds and make progress impossible. The technique itself offers many possibilities, if used carefully.

Fig 201. *Ribbing, partial knit in a number of contrasting patterns.*

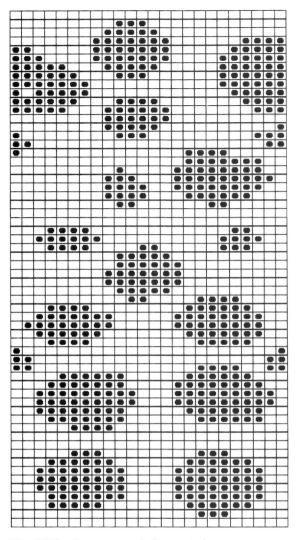

Fig 202. *Pattern graph for spot design.*

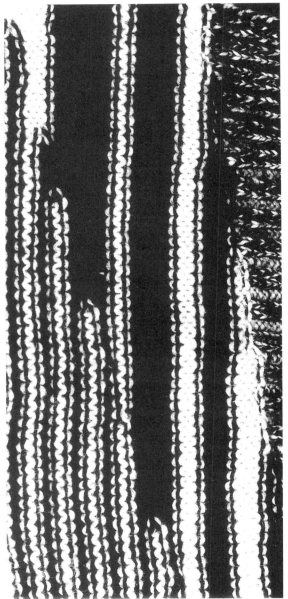

Fig 203. *Partial knit ribbing, with purl-facing stripes.*

The linker (fig 204)
This can be used to create horizontal and vertical ridges, as well as being used as a seaming device. It is also possible to apply trims using a linker.

Quilted surfaces
Wadding sold for dressmaking and furnishing uses can be applied to the back of a piece of knitting by machine sewing, giving a quilted effect.

Fig 204. *Linked ridges.*

Fig 205. *Quilted pleats.*

Do remember that if you are making a garment, the quilting fabric takes up space. A medium-size jacket can mysteriously become a small size if you don't allow for this.

Padded pleats (fig 205)
Make pleats in the normal way, but before picking up the base row, insert a strip of wadding or several strands of thick yarn. This can be combined with quilting to produce a relief effect.

Tubes
Lengths of knitted tubing can be made on a single-bed machine using the slip setting in one direction, and knitting in the opposite direction.

These can then be applied as a decorative feature either by hand or using the linker (see fig 114 on page 96).

Swiss darning and beads (fig 206)
An embroidery stitch which duplicates the appearance of a knitted stitch. It can be used to outline and accentuate areas of knit. It is also useful with 2-colour knitting if a third colour needs to be introduced in an area of pattern. This stitch is referred to as duplicate stitch in some manuals.

Other hand-embroidery stitches can be used such as chain stitch and cross stitch. Beads, too, can be added to create richly decorated surfaces.

163

Fig 206. *Embroidered beaded surface on a 2-colour patterned knit.*

CHAPTER 9
Developing previous samples and experiments

This final chapter not only looks at ways of developing previous samples and experiments, but also suggests ways of extending them to suit a number of varied functions from garments and accessories to domestic furnishings.

A good starting point is to take a small group of related pattern samples. Alter first the colour combinations in the light of new sources of inspiration, next the yarn type, and finally the gauge and weights can be adapted to suit new circumstances. For instance, a winter coat will necessarily be constructed in bulkier yarns than a summer sweater, even though the pattern may be from the same source.

As you become more familiar with the many possibilities open to you as a designer of knitted garments, information from diverse groups of samples can be cross-referenced, combining patterns that could possibly go together, even though the initial design experiments stem from totally different sources. For example, an all-over small-scale repeat pattern from one group, when knitted in another yarn or colour, may be a perfect complement to a large-scale intarsia motif from another project.

Experiment by laying out groups of mixed samples on a large table top. Rearrange them into different groupings, working intuitively at first. You may hit upon some surprise combinations which you would never have considered using a more logical approach. Continue by knitting up ribs or areas of texture in tuck or slip-stitch to complement the patterned sections. It could be an idea for a matching skirt or a plain sweater to complement a highly patterned cardigan.

I will suggest a number of links between one technique and another, looking at possible designs for individual garments using one or more methods. For example, a co-ordinated range of knitting could be knitted which could either be one complete outfit, perhaps including a coat or jacket, a skirt or matching undersweater. Alternatively, a group of accessories could be worked or sweaters for family sport or leisure

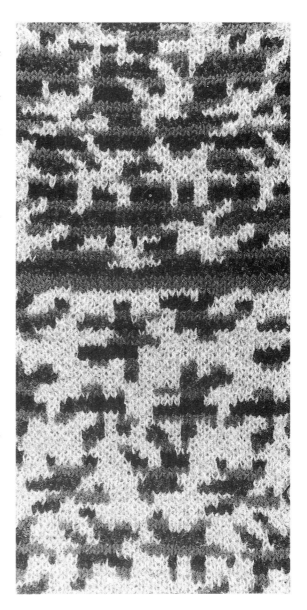

Fig 207. *Machine-knitted Jacquard.*

wear. Each could use a standard yarn worked within one colour story, but knitted in different patterns (all geometric, for example). A suggested range of alternative colourings could also be offered.

Another example of combining techniques is to create an exclusive jacket worked in intarsia over the complete bodice, on the chunky-gauge machine, while the sleeves are knitted in double-bed patterned Jacquard on the standard-gauge machine. A simple co-ordinating ribbed or textured skirt or a close-fitting dress, picking out a main colour, would complete the outfit.

Various techniques nearly always need to be applied when designing a group of garments, giving the necessary balances and changes of scale to areas of pattern and complementary sections of plain or textured knit. Ribs and hems need to be considered in this context. You may also decide, if you are a hand-knitter, to design a lightweight machine-knit sweater to complement a hand-knit jacket (see figs 207 and 208).

Whatever the design, choose a solution where the technique, gauge and yarn-type are each suited to the purpose and style of the garment. For example a close-fitting garment without an opening must have elasticity. A sweater for winter or general outdoor wear needs to be knitted in yarns which will trap a layer of air for warmth. A work-wear sweater must be of a resilient, hard-wearing yarn. Conversely, a glamorous evening sweater should be knitted in fine or cool yarns that are not too warm and bulky for indoor wear.

It is important to understand the main qualities and characteristics of the various fibres available to the knitter. The ultimate choice of yarn should not only be based on its aesthetic appeal, but should also take into account the intended function of the garment. Performance requirements must be considered – durability, comfort, warmth and softness of the yarn; its ability to absorb moisture; how much drop can be expected from a particular yarn, or whether or not the yarn is a good conductor of heat.

It is also necessary to determine if the yarn needs to be machine or handwashed, or whether it must be dry-cleaned (not really suitable for children's wear). Look also at the qualities of drape and ability to dispel creases easily.

Taking the most popular natural fibres used by the knitter I offer a brief summary of their main character-istics, but refer you to the many specialist reference books available on this subject, and suggest further reading (see Bibliography). A selected range of yarns suitable for machine knitting is shown in fig 14.

Cotton will absorb moisture and is a good conduc-tor of heat. Garments knitted in this fibre are suited to summerwear, or humid conditions generally. How-ever, cotton does have a tendency to feel clammy in the wrong type of climate. It is a smooth yarn, cool to the touch and generally regarded as non-irritant to those with sensitive skin conditions.

Since it is a dense, heavy yarn, cotton hangs well when knitted but does have a tendency to drop. The fibres are smooth and rounded and do not cling together as do those of wool, which are rough and scaly. You should try to estimate drop before knitting a complete garment, although this is not always easy

Fig 208. *A hand knit using slip stitch.*

to do. I always let a full-length sample garment hang for a few days, taking measurements before and after.

If, for example, you are knitting a long skirt, perhaps leave it to hang before attaching the waistband. If the skirt is part of a dress, let it hang before attaching the bodice. It is much easier to unravel a few unwanted rows at this stage than to do so when the garment is complete. An alternative is to use a yarn consisting of cotton blended with other fibres.

Cotton is easy to wash, but because it retains moisture it can take a long time to dry. The fibres are reasonably strong and durable but cotton knitwear can be prone to mildew if kept in damp conditions for any length of time – a consequence of its moisture-absorbing properties. Prolonged exposure to sunlight can eventually weaken the fibre, but on the plus side, cotton, unlike wool, is not prone to attack by moth larvae.

When considering wool, one can say that it drapes well and has superb insulating qualities, making woollen knitwear warm to wear and soft to the touch. The fibres do not readily transmit heat, so the body of the wearer stays warm – important in wintry conditions. Air is trapped in the hairy fibres which, due to their natural crimp and resilience, stand away from each other.

Wool can also absorb an excess of moisture without feeling cold and clammy, unlike cotton (compare the feel of cotton and wool fabrics). It possesses a natural elasticity and resilience which makes knitting an easy proposition if the correct type of wool is chosen. These properties also mean that, unlike cotton, creases are easily lost.

When knitting a garment for a client or friend, check that wool does not irritate their skin. Some people find it impossible to wear the rougher, coarser homespun-type wools, but may find that a fine, soft wool is acceptable – although it must be remembered that these may not be as durable.

In general, each fibre-type has its own particular advantages and drawbacks, which need to be considered in conjunction with the function and appearance of the garment that you intend to knit, and you should also bear in mind the person who will ultimately be wearing the item.

Wool does have certain problems associated with it. First, it can felt and shrink when excessive heat and/or friction is applied to the surface. This can happen during washing or when the wool is next to the skin. As has already been mentioned, wools can be itchy, and can cause allergic reactions in sensitive individ-

uals. Always check with a potential recipient of your knitwear that this will not be a problem.

Some soft wools can be susceptible to 'pilling' – a process in which small fluffy balls accumulate on the surface of the garment.

Finally, moths like wool. Take precautions against this, especially if you may be storing cones of woollen yarn for any length of time.

There are many other fibres on the market, either blends or mixes or 100 per cent pure. A vast range of synthetic yarns complement the natural fibres, and are often mixed to improve certain characteristics, or to produce a less expensive but still good quality yarn. Speciality hair fibres, for example, include mohair, cashmere, camel, llama and alpaca, vicuna, horse, rabbit, fox, chinchilla and racoon.

Generally speaking these yarns are expensive, as they are produced in smaller quantities than wool or cotton, but they give an exclusive and unusual appearance to high-quality knitwear. They can also be mixed with other natural fibres (see my sample range in luxury and exotic fibres). Very often it is possible to purchase blends and mixes of these yarns. Celandine Yarns and Many-A-Mickle can both supply them (see list of stockists).

Linen and silk are also both suitable for knitting. Silk possesses strength, resilience and elasticity combined with a high lustre, softness and a superb drape. Linen can be coarse and difficult to knit, unless it is spun with wool, for example, or cotton.

The wholly synthetic (man-made) yarns include acrylics, acetates, polyesters, nylon and related fibres, and metallics and tinsel threads. There are also 'regenerated' fibres such as viscose rayon. This is a cellulose fibre produced from (for example) wood pulp. Cellulose is a natural substance, but is chemically reformed or regenerated to produce rayon.

It is important to try to understand the main characteristics of a variety of yarns in order to make a completely successful garment from scratch. Each one needs to be studied in relationship to the function of the garment.

For example, some synthetic yarns can be very easily distorted by excess heat and stress. Instead of shrinking like wool, bagginess results, causing unsightly seating on skirts, baggy knees and elbows, and ribbing which has lost its elasticity. Incidentally, this latter problem can be alleviated by incorporating a fine, almost invisible knitting elastic into the rib.

A child's sweater is best knitted in a durable, yet comfortable fibre that is machine washable and not too expensive, as it will be soon outgrown. Try using some of the Superwash wools. These are shrink-resistant, machine washable, and reasonably priced for their quality. A good range of colours is available from King Kole Yarns.

My own view is that if you are producing a handmade piece of knitwear, go for the best quality yarns of a suitable type that you can afford. Think of all the hours of work that go into making one garment, and compare it to the cost of, say, $\frac{1}{2}$ kg of good-quality wool. You might spend hours on a beautiful piece of intarsia work, and have it bagging or pilling after one or two outings because you have used cheap and inadequate yarn. This really would be false economy. It is simply not worth the effort expended in making such a piece to see it fall apart soon after, and it can discourage further ventures.

It is important to note the ease with which certain yarns can be knitted on the machine. Generally, yarns that have the most resilience are the easiest to knit. Wool's natural elasticity compensates for the perhaps slightly erratic or jerky movements of the machine's carriage made by the inexperienced knitter.

Yarns that possess little natural give (for example linen or cotton) or which have a pronounced twist can initially be a problem for the novice, showing unsightly pulls or visible variations in tension – usually the result of unsteady movements of the carriage across the needle bed. The answer to this is to knit slowly until you become familiar with the yarn you are using.

If you find that the yarn is constantly snarling up, and twisting back on itself or around the tension assembly, stop using it and substitute another. Some yarns with a high twist are unsuitable for machine-knitting as they do have a tendency to twist back on themselves, unless placed under a very high tension.

Another associated problem comes from placing a yarn with a high twist adjacent to a softspun lightweight yarn in the tension assembly. This also causes snarling up, and consequent pulls and dropped stitches.

Occasionally a yarn may simply have been over-twisted during manufacture, and this can cause the above problems to crop up. You may find this happening if you purchase seconds or unspecified mill-ends, where the quality is not always guaranteed.

In conclusion, however brilliant the surface pattern and colour content are in their conception and aesthetic qualities, the choice of yarn and stitch structure must suit the function of the garment and the knitting process used. The design process *must* take these considerations into account. The ultimate

success of the garment is heavily dependent on a successful marriage of all these factors.

Before considering the details of particular colour combinations, and the specific type of design to be used, one or two general points need to be addressed. How to find a suitable garment shape? Is it necessary to draft a new pattern from scratch, or can existing patterns be altered to suit?

I think the answers depend very much on individual requirements and capabilities. The subject of pattern-cutting is outside the scope of this book, suitable titles being suggested in the bibliography. There are many published patterns for hand and machine knitting, both old and new, with linear diagrams of flat garment shapes, usually displaying the necessary measurements. These can be adapted to suit your own requirements, changing only the details of style – or not even those.

Try to build up a personal collection of varied, yet simple, shapes – noting down the original knitting technique used for a particular style. The easiest method of conversion is to transfer the shape to a charting device (either half-scale or full size depending upon your model) and knit the appropriate tension square in your own yarns, to suit your own design. This will establish the correct stitch ruler to be used alongside the row setting.

A problem which may occur is in visualizing how the all-over pattern will appear when knitted on a full size garment. It will take on quite a different appearance from a small size sample. Inexperienced designers may be surprised at the effect – for example sections of pattern and/or colour groupings may appear too strong when knitted *en masse*.

Sometimes patterns do not read as you would have expected, for instance certain colours which appear tonally different in close-up merge into one when seen from a distance. This can make some areas of patterning look indistinct and unbalanced.

To try to solve some of these problems I attempt to visualize how the complete width and length of a sweater front might appear. If, for example, the total number of stitches to be cast on is 144, and you are using a 24 stitch repeat system, then the main pattern unit would be repeated six times in all. Obviously, if the main pattern was a factor of 24 stitches, say a 6 stitch repeat – then the pattern would repeat 24 times over the complete front.

The same calculations apply to rows. If you know roughly how many rows are needed for the complete front, similar deductions can be made. You can also use a photocopier to reduce or expand a section of pattern to its actual size; this will depend on tension – how many stitches and rows per centimetre/inch.

Make several copies of the pattern and stick them together, using sellotape on the back or invisible tape on the front, to make a mock-up of the proposed garment. Intarsia-type patterns can be drawn up to scale on full-size pattern pieces made from newsprint, lining paper, or some other inexpensive paper. Colours can be roughly blocked in. This will give you, the designer, an idea of how the finished article may look.

The final section of this chapter examines ways of putting groups of samples together for single garments or outfits. These are only suggestions and a method to use. Make your own combinations work

for you. You should soon be on the way to producing individually designed pieces, bearing the stamp of your own personality.

Creating exotic patterned surfaces

In these samples, unusual, exotic and luxurious fibres are combined with images based on tropical fish. The designs and surfaces change in scale, texture and weight for use on either jackets and cardigans with coordinating undersweaters, or vest-tops. All the Alpacas used in these samples are, unless otherwise stated, obtainable from Many-A-Mickle (see list of suppliers).

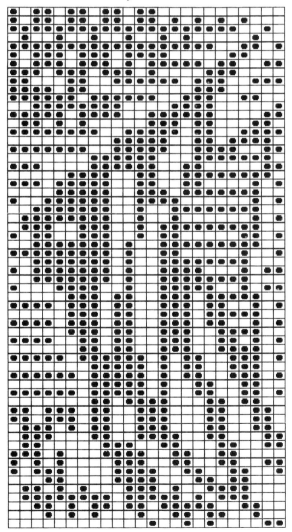

Fig 209. *Pattern graph for fish design.*

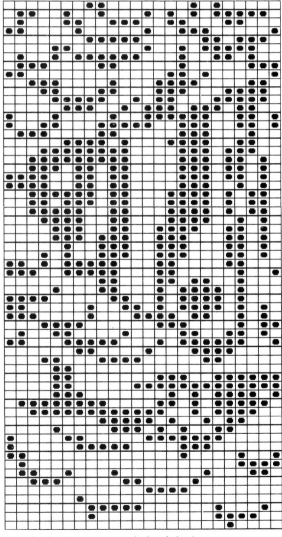

Fig 210. *Pattern graph for fish design.*

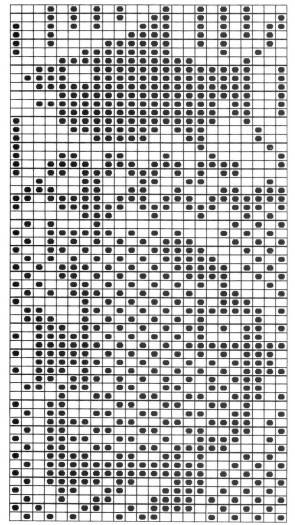

Fig 211. *Pattern graph for fish design.*

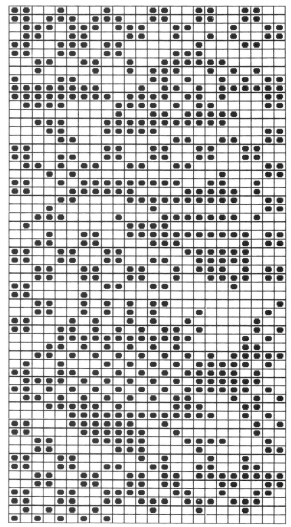

Fig 212. *Pattern graph for fish design.*

Sample 1 (fig 213)

This sample uses a soft, white Angora (available from Yeoman yarns) to complement three brown brushed Alpacas. The surface is raised by the use of a teasel brush (taking care not to pull the stitches) after the knitting has been removed from the machine. Some areas are left relatively flat, while others are fully brushed.

This sample is knitted at Tension 10 on a fine-gauge machine using single-bed two-colour knit over 60 stitches. I envisage the sample developing into a warm, yet lightweight, cardigan or special sweater for outdoor occasions.

Sample 2 (fig 214)

The design of this sample based on Angel Fish, combining brushed Alpaca (cream) with unusual mixes of yarn from Celandine Yarns. Two shades of 50% Mink and 50% Lambswool, and one shade of 50% Racoon and 50% Lambswool form the pattern in muted shades of brown-grey, green-grey and pink-grey.

The sample is knitted at Tension 8 over 60 stitches on a fine gauge machine. This forms a closer knit than the previous sample. The Alpaca sections are brushed up.

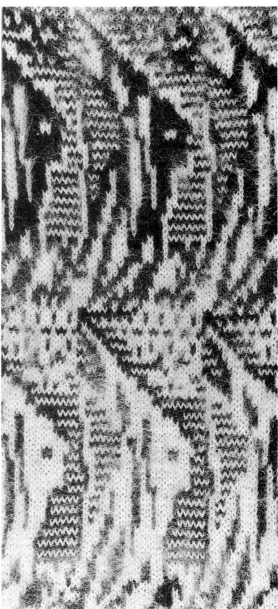

Fig 213. *Sample 1, knitted in angora and alpaca yarns.*

Fig 214. *Sample 2, knitted in alpaca, mink, lambswool and rayon.*

171

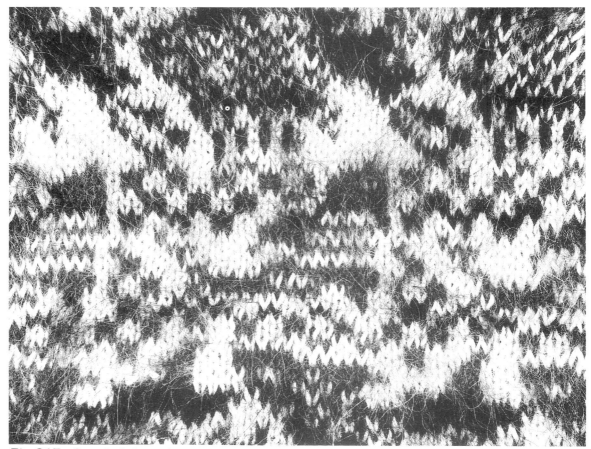

Fig 215. *Sample 3, knitted in alpacas alone.*

Sample 3 (fig 215)
Using smaller patterns, this sample is constructed to form a more substantial close-knitted fabric worked in an Alpaca DK from Twilleys (98% Alpaca, 2% Acrylic) used as a background to dark, mid, and light brown brushed Alpaca patterning.

It is worked at Tension 10 over 60 stitches, on a standard gauge machine. The weight and structure would suit a warm outdoor sweater.

A group of three samples follow which experiment with various combinations of luxury yarns; some smooth and reflective in surface quality – others matt or hairy in character (fig 216).

Sample 4
The first sample uses a silk (from HT Gaddum & Co) in black for the fish pattern, while the background is worked in close coloured stripes in the following from Celandine: 50% Racoon/50% Lambswool 4-ply in a neutral brown-grey, 50% Mink/50% Lambswool in two muted shades of grey-green and grey-pink.

This pattern could either be knitted as an all-over repeat for a lightweight sweater or be used as a border for a loose-fitting cardigan, or the yoke of a sweater with the remainder of the garment knitted in a single plain colour or a small overall pattern perhaps of birdseye type spots.

Fig 216. *Samples 4, 5 and 6, knitted in various luxury yarns, including silks, alpacas, lambswool.*

Sample 5
The next sample in this group uses a dark brown brushed-up Alpaca for the pattern, against a background of close coloured stripes in camel-coloured 50% Fox/50% Lambswool, a grey coloured 50% Chinchilla/50% Fox mix, and finally a grey-brown 50% Racoon/50% Lambswool 4-ply (all these available from Celandine Yarns).

This would work well as a border pattern on a cardigan either as a vertical band on both fronts and/ or as a horizontal band above the sleeve and body ribbing. The remainder of the garment could be knitted in the dark brown Alpaca, or the camel Fox/ Lambswool mix.

Sample 6
Finally, a blue silk (from Gaddum's) sample worked alongside the same exotic fibre yarns used in the background of sample 5. A loosefitting, lightweight cardigan is suggested with an undersweater to match

in the same yarns but with a different all-over pattern still based on the fish theme.

Samples 7 and 8 (fig 217)
Two samples in different weights combine to suggest a fine vest and a warm lightweight cardigan. A fine black, grey and white sample is knitted using a small pattern at Tension 4 over 60 stitches, producing a delicate piece of knitting. The yarns used are dark grey 50% Suri Alpaca/50% Lambswool mix, together with a black Cigno yarn from Yeoman against a cream 50% Silk/30% Cotton/20% Acrylic mix, and a cream Cigno. The more substantial sample worked in a bolder design uses a black silk from HT Gaddum, and a grey and two shades of brown in brushed Alpaca.

All the samples in this section so far use one technique but in a variety of yarns and tensions. Luxury yarns and the intarsia technique can produce exotic patterned surfaces. However, an intarsia motif could be used as a repetitive image using non-repetitive areas of colour or texture – or as a single

173

Fig 217. *Samples 7 and 8. Two sample ideas for coordinating fabric knitting in contrasting weights. Lightweight sample is knitted in 50% suri alpaca and 50% lambswool, mixed with a fine black mohair-type yarn. The heavier weight sample uses silk and alpaca.*

image for use against sections of plain knit in luxury fibres (fig 218).

Ribbing and areas of textured knit could also be included. For example, the main body of a cardigan could be patterned, whereas the sleeves and a coordinating skirt could be in a rib or a small tuck-stitch pattern using the same yarn and echoing the design characteristics from the main patterned section.

Top right **Fig 218.** *Pattern graph for intarsia motif.*

Figs 219–222 makes links through colour. The combination I chose to work around involved purple and ochre as the dominant colours, applied to solid and mixed colours in varying combinations.

In conclusion, your preliminary decision about what sort of design, pattern and techniques to employ needs to be based on, first, who or what the finished piece is for and second, the type of piece you intend to produce, be it garment, item of furnishing or whatever. For example, the piece could be for:

Country casuals.
Sophisticated evening wear.
Young, fun disco wear.
Children's wash-and-wear sweaters.
Active sportswear.
Daywear for the career woman.
A commission for an outsize ladies' cardigan.
A collection of co-ordinated garments and accessories for an upmarket store.
Something to indulge yourself with.
Something to indulge your grandmother with.
A bedspread with matching cushions.

The possibilities are endless but whatever you are involved with consideration ought to be given to colour, scale and type of decorative imagery; suitability of a particular collection of yarns; weight of garment; ease of washing; suitability of technique.

The more sampling and designing you do, the easier it will become to assess whether your knitting really is suitable for the particular use you have in mind. Further questions you should ask yourself before embarking on a finished piece are:

1. Is the scale and distribution of surface pattern and decoration suited to the overall shape and size of the piece?
2. Do I want a tight or loose fit (if a garment)? Is there enough ease and elasticity to allow for comfort?
3. Is the combination of yarn weight and knitting technique suitable for the intended purpose (Daywear, children's wear, etc)? For example, is 2-strand fairisle with floats on the reverse the most suitable for clothing for an active child, or would Intarsia or Jacquard (double-bed) be more practical? Maybe Jacquard would be too heavy and stiff in a particular type of yarn.

Bottom right **Fig 219.** *Sample ideas for panels in jackets or coats.*

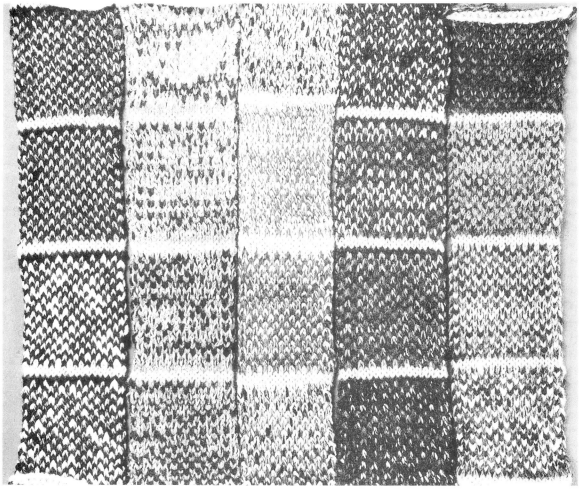

Fig 220. *Sample ideas in a small birdseye pattern suited to coordinating sweaters with Figs 219, 221 or 222.*

Experiments and limitations

Pure experimentation is a joy and also a luxury at times if you are busy producing work commercially. But you should endeavour to find the time to develop and try out new design ideas, combinations of yarns and stitches and so on, otherwise your work can become stale and repetitive. Of course, there is also scope for experiment within the bounds of a particular project. A good designer should be able to create original and exciting work that also suits the intended purpose. Designing a particular piece should not inhibit your creativity. You should see it as a challenge to tailor your experiments to the production of a set piece of work.

Versatility of decorative pattern

Can the same example of surface pattern be used, for instance, on both an item of evening wear and something like a daytime sweater? Quite possibly the answer is yes. The way in which you use colour and type of yarn can completely change the feel of a pattern so that it works in a wide range of contexts. This is not always the case, of course, since a design for a small child's sweater is unlikely to be convertible to something applicable to daywear for a career woman. It all depends on the kind of pattern. Non-figurative geometric motifs can be extremely versatile in this respect.

Right **Fig 221.** *Beaded panel.*

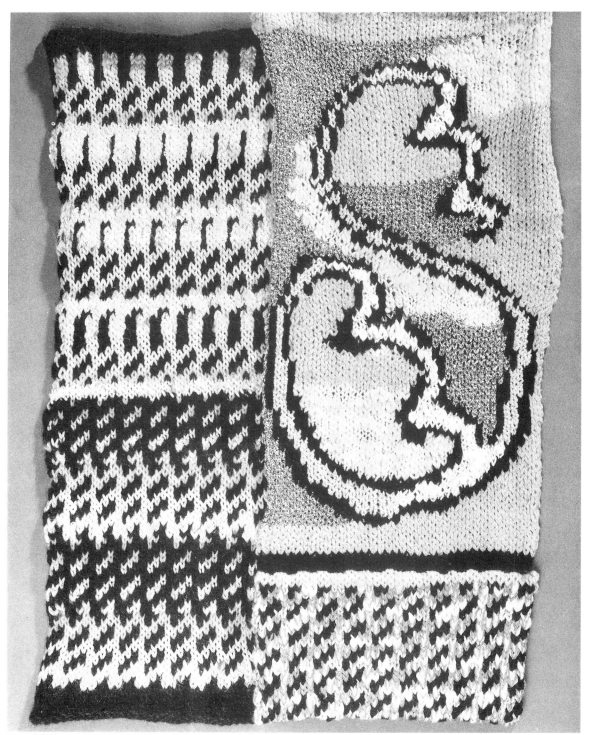

Fig 222. *Intarsia motif with a coordinating 2-colour patterned knit. Sample ideas for a medium weight sweater and cardigan.*

By the time you have worked your way through the examples included in this book you should be armed with enough information to design and knit a great variety of exciting and decorative patterns suitable for all occasions. Don't worry, however, if not everything you make is a raving success. The most experienced and professional designer has an occasional off-day. The trick is to profit from any mistakes you make by working out where you went wrong so that you can avoid the same trap in future. Put the offending item aside for a while and have a look at it on a later date with a fresh mind. The chances are that you will see very quickly where the problems lie. Don't be afraid to ask for advice or comment from other, perhaps more experienced, knitters. You don't *have* to take any notice and you might gain some insight from a different viewpoint. Most of all, enjoy the satisfaction of having designed a piece of knitting from scratch through to a finished article, and the subsequent desire to push the limits even further in your next project.

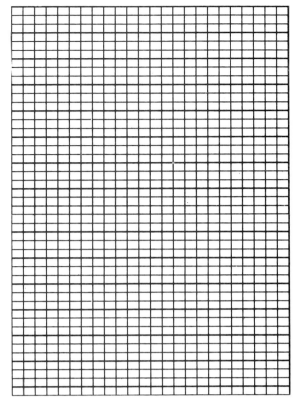

Fig 223. *Blank sheet of proportional graph-paper.*

APPENDICES

Computer Aided Design and Machine Knitting

New technology can offer the creative knitter invaluable aids to solving design problems quickly and efficiently. Some systems allow patterns to be designed on the computer and then stored on magnetic disc to be used when required to program an electronic machine directly. In this instance the pattern does not have to be transferred to mylar sheet; there is a direct link between the computer and the knitting machine (see Masterknit and Brother PPD110).

Other software is intended purely as a design tool for working out and experimenting with repetitive patterns on the screen of the computer. Again, this information can be stored on disc or tape for future reference. The mylar sheet or punchcard can be prepared either directly from the screen or from a print-out, should you have access to a suitable printer.

I have listed some products which you may find of interest, particularly if you own a home computer.

Puncher (by Mark Lancaster a knitting machine punch-card designer

This program runs on the Atari ST series of computers, and enables you to experiment with different punchcard designs and colour schemes, without actually punching any cards or doing any knitting. You can also view the designs as they would appear on simple garment shapes, and make print-outs of the patterns if you have a printer. The designs can be stored on disc for future use. The program is available from Mark Lancaster, 84 Redfern Avenue, Hounslow, Middlesex TW4 5L2.

Punchcard 24 (by David Jackman)

Versions of this program are available for the following computers; Spectrum, Commodore C64 and Amstrad CPC series. As in the previous case, 2-colour designs can be adapted and experimented with prior to actually punching a card. Various colourways can be tried out. Your designs can be stored on disc alongside pre-recorded ones, allowing the knitter to create many exciting composite patterns. Another very useful feature allows for single-bed Jacquard to be converted to double Jacquard. This software is available from Knitsoft, 1 Valley Close, Yarm, Cleveland.

Masterknit 200

This is a complete system for use with the Knitmaster 550, 560 and 580 in conjunction with a BBC computer. Unique designs from 2 to 200 stitches wide can be created on screen using for example the AMX Art Drawing package. Pictures made in this way can be transferred directly from the computer to the knitting machine. There is also a garment knitting package which allows the user to manipulate garment shapes on the screen and position them over a design. The program provides on-screen knitting instructions. A garment designing facility is also provided. A version for the Spectrum computer should be available in the near future. Details can be obtained from Clwyd Technics (Educational Computing Specialists), Antelope Industrial Estate, Rhydymuyn, Nr Mold, Clwyd CH7 5JH.

Classic Pattern Writer by Terry Mason

This is for use with the Spectrum home computer, and is supplied in cassette form. A series of garment pattern shapes is included, for example a V-neck, Raglan inset sleeves short or long. You can knit to a standard size or to your own measurements. The program asks for the number of rows and stitches from your tension swatch (which you must knit in the correct yarn, pattern and stitch size), and then works out the amount of rows and stitches needed for a particular design. On-screen instructions alongside a visual representation of the garment make things easy to follow. You can also make a print-out to work from if you have a printer. This program is available from T. Mason, 15 Inishmoyne Green, Antrim, Northern Ireland BT4 14J2.

General purpose software

In general terms it is possible to create grids to design on to using some of the general-purpose drawing and design software available for specific computers, for example *Degas Elite* (for the Atari ST series) or *Image* and AMX Art for the BBC machine.

The Pattern Programming Device (PPD11O) by Brother

This accessory allows the creation of designs on screen (a domestic television is suitable), and has a facility for storing the pattern for future use. The PPD is connected to either the Brother 9501 or the 940 when you are ready to knit, and the information is then transferred on to the machine. Patterns can be stored on the PPD or on disc. Again it is possible to make print-outs if you have a suitable printer. More information can be obtained from Brother (Knitting Machine Division), Strepley Street, Guide Bridge, Audenshaw, Manchester M34 5JD (Tel 061-330 6531).

Suppliers of Knitting Machines and Accessories

Brother Knitting Machines
Shepley Street
Guide Bridge
Audenshaw
Manchester M34 5JD

1. KH836 Punchcard model combines with a KR850 or KR830 ribber. A full-scale charting device KL116 Knitleader and a separate intarsia carriage are also available.

2. KH230 and KH260 are chunky knitters. The KH260 has a 24-stitch repeat system, and can be used in conjunction with a ribber KR260 to produce double-bed Jacquard using the KRC900 colour-changer. Both the KH260 and KH230 use the KL116 knitleader. Intarsia is also possible. The KH200 needs a separate intarsia carriage (KA2600).

3. KH890 and KH891 are more advanced standard-gauge punchcard machines which use either the KR850 or KR830 ribbing attachment. The KH891 has a built-in knitleader. The KL116 knitleader can be attached to the KH890. Intarsia carriages are available.

4. KH9501 is the Brother advanced electronic machine which is capable of knitting a single repeat anywhere from 1 to 200 stitches wide. Patterns can be doubled in width and length, switched between negative and positive, knitted upside down as a reflection or as a single motif. The most unusual feature is the facility to knit two different patterns on the same line. Attachments included the KR850 ribber, KL116 knitleader, single and double bed colour-changers, and the pattern programming device (see section on computer aided design). A training video presented by Janet Nabney and Wendy Nelson is also available from Brother for the KH950.

Knitmaster
39–45 Cowleaze Road
Kingston upon Thames
Surrey KT2 6DT

1. Knitmaster 700 – a punchcard machine for new knitters which can be linked with the SRP-50 ribber.

An instruction book is complemented by a tuition tape. Intarsia is a standard feature of this machine and is combined with a full-scale knit radar. A single colour changer YC-6 can be used for both single and double bed patterns.

2. Knitmaster 155. A fully automatic chunky punchcard machine with a 12-stitch repeat which can be combined with the SR-155 ribber and the KR-7 knit radar. Another accessory is the intarsia carriage for picture knitting.

3. Knitmaster Zippy 90 is an ideal chunky machine for new knitters. An intarsia carriage is available (AG10).

4. Design Master Electronic – this advanced machine can deal with small pattern repeats or massive non-repeating single motif picture knits 200 stitches wide by 1000 rows long. Many pattern variations are available, such as reversing the colours, doubling the length and width, mirroring the pattern. Single bed patterns can be transformed into double bed Jacquard. A ribber (SRP60N) is available, as is an automatic colour changer YC6, and an intarsia carriage. Another new accessory is the PEI design controller which allows you to design patterns up to 200 stitches by 1000 rows, which can be stored on a memory card.

Pfaff (Britain) Ltd
Pfaff House
East Street
Leeds SL59 8EH

Pfaff sell two models of knitting machine; the Duomatic 80 and the electronic 6000E. Both machines are 5mm gauge, and are sold complete with stand and 4-way colour changer. They are true double bed knitting machines.

The two main beds each have the same patterning abilities and either can do the work of the ribber. On the Duomatic, patterns can be produced either by using the pushers set manually, or by using the punchcard system called the Deco. Duomatic punchcards have a 40-stitch repeat, and the cardholder can be placed anywhere along the needle bed. Another accessory is the Pfaff Form Computer which tells you step by step exactly what to do during, for example, garment shaping. The Pfaff Electronic 6000 has built-in patterns as well as the facility to memorise the user's own designs. Patterns can be expanded independantly in horizontal and vertical dimensions or both at once, up to a ×99 enlargment. Patterns can be designed to use the full width of the machine. A motif can be positioned wherever desired as well as being mirrored, rotated, reversed and superimposed. Automatic intarsia is possible on the electronic model.

Toyota Sewing and Knitting
Aisin (UK) Ltd
34 High Street
Bromley
Kent BR1 1EA

Toyota market a range of machines upon which patterns can be produced either by manual selection of the needles or via a punchcard. The KR506 ribber will fit all of their current standard gauge machines.
1. Model KS858/KS777 combines a 12-stitch repeat punchcard with manual selection of 12 stitches. Linked with a ribber it is possible to produce reversible knitting (Simulknit). An intarsia carriage is also available, as is a full-scale knit tracer.
2. Model KS950 has a 24-stitch repeat punchcard, and again features Simulknit when linked with the KR506 ribber. A colour changer, knit tracer and intarsia carriage are also available.
3. Toyota also produce an electric linking machine A500 which can either be used for seaming, attaching bands and braids, or producing an ornamental chain stitch.

Singer (Knitting Machine Dept)
255 High Street
Guildford
Surrey

Several single bed machines are available which use a push-button needle selection system. Singer also market double bed electronics models type Memo 600 and Memomatic 2310. Memo 600 is computer based and uses transparent sheets upon which the design is drawn. The Memomatic 2310 is an update of the 600, and has a pattern width of 60 stitches. A pattern driver (Singer's charting device) can also be attached. Singer also market a chunky machine the

Designer 2. They produce a newsletter for knitting clubs, classes, and tutors which can be obtained from Kim Howard (Knitting Services Coordinator), SDL Ltd, Grafton Way, Basingstoke, Hampshire RG22 6HZ.

B. Hague & Co Ltd
Colwick
Nottingham

Hague Domestic Linkers models DIO/DIOE for making up and decorative work such as producing pin-tucks on patterned knit or on the reverse side of plain or tuck stitch in vertical or horizontal directions. Braidings, sequins and beads already joined by a linking thread and cards can be applied using this device.

Tricot Products Ltd
Unit 3
Polham Lane
Somerton
Somerset TA11 65P

This firm markets a range of machine knitting accessories, for example:
1. Intarsia carriage for Duomatic machines.
2. Intarsia multi-yarn brake.
3. Tricot design charts – asymmetric graph-paper in three grades for single gauge or chunky yarns.

Dawson's Grid – available from:
287 Brompton Road
London SW32 2DY
Tel 01-589 0772

Graphic Knitting Supplies:
Mrs Gregg
2 Pinewood Park
Drumbo
Co Down
Northern Ireland

Machine Knitting and Design Centre
High Cross House
High Cross
Aldenham
Watford WD2 8BN

Videos by Kamalini for Brother ribbers, including one on double bed Jacquard.

List of Suppliers

Most yarn firms will make a charge for shade cards. Prices and available qualities can be obtained from individual companies.

Texere Yarns
College Mill
Barkerend Road
Bradford, Yorks
BD3 9AG

A most comprehensive cross section of yarns including 100% pure new wools, alpacas, mohairs, cottons, viscose lurex mixes, a wide selection of natural coloured silks, slub cottons, fancy knops and spiral yarns, woollenspun yarns, dyed silks, crepe yarns. A standard shade card is supplemented with temporary additions from time to time.

Yeoman Yarns
89 Leicester Road
Kibworth
Leicestershire

Yarns from the UK, Italy, France and Switzerland covering a wide range of types and blends: fine mohair blends (Elsa), 4-ply 100% slub cotton (Flamme), chenille, acrylic and viscose mixes (Grigna), 4-ply 100% mercerised cotton (Cannele), fancy metallic yarns and angora. An excellent variety of good quality yarns.

Brockwell Wools
Stansfield Mill
Triangle
Sowerby Bridge
West Yorks

Single ends of yarn are held in stock, and can be twisted to the plys required by the knitter. Yarns held in stock include Botany wool, mercerised cotton, lambswools, Lurex, and brushed mohair. Minimum order 350 gm approx.

Celandine Yarns
44 Kirkgate
Otley
West Yorks

Interesting and unusual pure luxury yarns. A joy to work with. They include mink, lambswool, chinchilla, racoon, fox, suri alpaca, superkid mohair, silk, cotton, combined in various mixes in subtle colours.

T. Forsell & Son Ltd
Blaby Road
South Wigston
Leicester

Recommended for machine knitting – Forsell 3-ply pure new wool, Sirocco – a 3-ply 80% acrylic and 20% wool, and Naturel – a 3-ply 80% wool and 20% alpaca.

H.T. Gaddum
3 Jordangate
Macclesfield
Cheshire SK10 1EF

This firm specializes in silk yarns and will deal directly with the public. Especially recommended is their Como 50/70 silk knitting yarn in a good range of colours.

Atkinson Designer Collection
Terry Mills
Osset
West Yorks

A good range of fancy and mixed yarns which are easy to knit. Examples include a 100% acrylic chenille, Hibiscus – a mix of cotton and viscose, Geneve – an acrylic and nylon mix, Twizzle – a lovely fine shaggy yarn, and many others.

King Kole Ltd
Merrie Mills
Old Souls Way
Bingley
West Yorks

DK and 4-ply 100% pure new wool, anti-tickle and machine-washable. They generally sell through stockists and mailorder companies.

Laidlaw & Fairgreave
Ladhope Mills
Galashiels
Selkirkshire
Scotland

A mail-order service for natural, fancy machine and hand knitting yarns. A very good colour range including Shetlands, Shetland/Donegal wool blends and some specialty yarns.

F.W. Bramwell & Co Ltd
Unit 5
Metcalf Drive
Altham Lane
Altham
Accrington

Look particularly at the 100% cotton which knits as a 2-ply (Montana), Silki – a 100% bright acrylic (good for very fine Jacquard). Other yarns include Tweedknit in a range of soft mixed colours, and a 100% acrylic which knits as a 4-ply, Artistic.

Jamieson & Smith
Shetland Wool Brokers
90 North Road
Lerwick
Shetland 2EL OP4

A comprehensive range of colours in 2-ply jumper weight Shetland. They also carry 2-ply lace weight, 4-ply Unst fleece yarns, Embo 3-ply yarns and 2-ply softspun chunky type yarn.

T.M. Hunter Ltd
Sutherland Wool Mills
Brora
Sutherland
Scotland

A stock service of Shetland in jumper and lace weight, plus double knitting weight and Aran.

Twilleys
Roman Mill
Stamford
Lincs

A good range including Lystwist 100% viscose, 100% Perlspun mercerised cotton, fine crochet cottons, 8-ply cottons (good on the chunky machine), goldfingering, and a denim yarn.

Many-A-Mickle
Hacking St
Darwen
Lancs

This firm specialises in natural yarns on cone. An excellent colour range which includes 100% pure new wool, Shetlands, and 100% Botany wool in 2/7's and 2/16's, also 4-ply pure new wool, brushed alpaca, a fleck tweed in many unusual shades, and ranges of both mercerised and slub cotton.

Nethy Products
Stewarton
Ayrshire
Scotland

Lambswool, Shetland, Shetland/cotton, mohair, and Donegal.

Pamela Wise
101–105 Goswell Road
London EC1V 7ER

A very comprehensive range of wools, cottons, silks, blends and mohair in may colours.

Other firms of interest:

J.C. Rennie & Co, Woollen spinners, Weavers Lane, Peterhead, Scotland AB4 65A (Shetland yarns).

J. Hyslop Bathgate & Co, Victoria Works, Galashiels, Scotland TD1 1NY (wools, mohair, spun silks).

Naturally Beautiful, Broadfield House, Dent, Cumbria LA10 STG (silks and cottons).

Holywell Textile Mills Ltd, Holywell, Clywd, North Wales CH8 7NU (Jacob knitting wools).

Huddersfield Mohair Mills, Rufford Road (off Scar Lane), Milnsbridge, Huddersfield HO3 4RC (various mohairs suited to handknit and chunky gauge knitting).

Look also at firms who generally produce yarns for hand-knitting – these may be suited to chunky machines.

Most of the large firms will sell through local stockists.

Emu Wools Ltd
Leeds Road
Greengates
Bradford
West Yorks

Patons & Baldwin
P O Box Darlington
Co Durham

Hayfields
Glusburn
Keighley
West Yorks

Argyll Wools Ltd
P O Box 15
Priestley Mills
Pudsey
West Yorks LS28 9LT

Pingouin
Station House
81–83 Fulham High Street
London SW6 3JW

Bibliography

1. Periodicals

These are useful for new products, yarns etc. as well as patterns.

Machine Knitting News published by Litharne Ltd.

Modern Machine Knitting from Modern Knitting Ltd.

Fashion and Craft from Blenheim Publications Ltd.

New Pins and Needles from Quarto International Ltd.

Modern Knitting Monthly from Machine Knitting Monthly Ltd.

Profitable Machine Knitting edited by Hazel Ratcliffe. Issued six times per year.

Knitting Machine Journal for Passap owners.

Knitting International – the leading technical journal for the hosiery, underwear, knitwear and knitted fabric industry.

Crafts which deals with the crafts scene generally. Six issues per year from 8 Waterloo Place, London SW1Y 4AT. Available from galleries and the occasional newsagent.

Nihon Vogue, Japanese machine knitting magazine

2. International Fashion Magazines

Most of these can be obtained from R D Franks Ltd, Market Place, Great Tichfield Street, London WIN 8EJ. Franks will send these to you if you send the money in advance, but be warned – some of them are very expensive as they are essentially trade magazines. Examples include:

International Textiles
Avante Garde
Pitti Filati
An Italian knitwear trade report presenting advanced information on new yarns, stitches, colours etc.
Maglieria Italiana
Advanced trends in fashion knitwear.
Vogue Knitting International
Burda – a range of magazines dealing with fashion aspects is published under this title.

Neve Mode
Children's clothes in knitting and crochet – age group 2–6.
Rivista Della Maglieria (RMI)
Knitwear fashions and advanced trends in knitwear for men and women.

3. Source Material for use in Designing your own Patterns

Bracken books, a division of Bestseller Pubications Ltd, produce a range of pattern books in a reasonable price range; some subject examples are:

William Morris designs and patterns.
Art Nouveau floral designs.
Abstract patterns and designs.
Art Deco interior and panel designs.
Abstract floral designs.
Heraldic designs.
Decorative alphabets plain and ornamental.

Portland House Books have a series of beautifully patterned Gift Wrap Books (as they are called) including:

Paisley designs
Oriental designs
English chintz floral designs
French floral designs
Art Deco designs
Art Nouveau designs

Belvedere Design Books have a range covering, for example:

Oriental flowers.
Decor.
Japanese flower motifs.
Lines and stripes in variation.

Belvedere Designer Notebooks cover, for example:
Chinese ceramics.
Japanese patterns.
Natural flowers.

Bibliography

Dover Books have many handbooks on decoration including:
The Style of Ornament (A Soltz)
Design for Artists and Craftsmen (L Wolchonok)
Handbook of Designs and Devices (C P Hornung)
Design Motifs of Ancient Mexico (J Encisco)
Primitive Art (Franz Boas)
The Hand book of Plant and Floral Ornament (R G Hatton)

Other useful source material can be found in the following publications. Check your local library for similar books.
Tribal Rugs (Jenny Housego) Scorpion Publications Ltd
Islamic Carpets from the Joseph V McMullan Collection Arts Council of Great Britain 1972
The Raoul Dufy Exhibition catalogue (including textiles) 1983/1984, Arts Council of Great Britain
Narrow Boat Painting (A J Lewery) David & Charles Publications
The Grammar of Ornament (Owen Jones) Omega Books Ltd
Celtic Art: The Methods of Construction (George Bain) Constable and Co. Ltd
Celtic Knot Work (Iain Bain) Constable and Co. Ltd
Textiles of Baluchistan (M.G. Konieczny) British Museum
Folk Costumes from Eastern Europe, Africa, Asia (Tilke)
Patterns in Nature (Peter S Stevens) Penguin (Peregrine)
Soviet Textile Design of the Revolutionary Period (I Yasinskaya) Thames & Hudson

Gold of the Pharaohs (catalogue – exhibition of treasures from Tanis), City of Edinburgh Museums and Art galleries
Hats from India (Rosemary Crill) Victoria and Albert Museum, 1985
Dictionary of Needlework (Caulfield and Saward) Hamlyn Books

3. Knitting Books

Yarns for the Knitter (Tessa Lorant) Thorn Press
Textile Properties and Behaviour in Clothing Use (E Miller) Batsford
The Art of Knitting (edited by Eve Harlow) Collins
The Complete Book of Traditional Fairisle Knitting (Sheila McGregor) Batsford
The Complete Book of Scandinavian Knitting (Sheila McGregor) Batsford
The Complete Book of Traditional Knitting (Rae Compton) Batsford
A History of Hand Knitting (Richard Rutt – Bishop of Leicester) Batsford.
Traditional Knitting (Sheila McGregor) Batsford
Traditional Knitting (Michael Pearson) Collins
Stitches in Time (Sue Bradley) Orbis
Designing for the Knitting Machine (Bea Poulter) Batsford
The Progressive Knitter (Maggie Whiting) Batsford
Nicely Knit Lines (Mary Louise Norman) – professional pattern drafting for machine knitters. Available from 'The Knitting Neuk', 32 Ashley Road, Aberdeen, Scotland

INDEX